Pass the Blessings!
(Ready, Set, Go)

By
Eveleaner Grant

Copyright © 2010 by Eveleaner Grant

Pass the Blessing!
Ready, Set, Go
by Eveleaner Grant

Printed in the United States of America

ISBN 9781609576561

All rights reserved solely by the author. The author guarantees all contents are original and do not infringe upon the legal rights of any other person or work. No part of this book may be reproduced in any form without the permission of the author. The views expressed in this book are not necessarily those of the publisher.

Unless otherwise indicated, Bible quotations are taken from The New International Version of the Bible. Copyright © 1996 The Zondervan Corporation; and The Compton's Interactive Bible - Compton's New Media, Inc. Copyright © 1996 Soft Key International, Inc.

Partial editing by Brenda Pitts

www.xulonpress.com

I dedicate this book to my husband, Lemuel, who loved me and the kids in such an unconditional way. I'm sorry for making things so hard but I thank God and you for sticking in there with me. I hope I have added to your life as you have added to mine. Thank you!

I especially dedicate this book to my children, Brandon, Basil and Amber, for loving your mother when she was so unlovable but you love me anyway. I made so many mistakes with you all. I want to say I am sorry and ask you to continue to forgive me. When you think of something else I have not apologized for, just let me know. I want the best for you and I want nothing I've done to stand in the way of your success in life. Thank you!

Also, I would like to dedicate this book to my mother, Carrie. I love you and I have so many fond memories of my childhood, teenage years and adulthood. Thank you!

Lastly, I would like to dedicate this book to Mrs. Joyce Alley who was a neighbor, dear friend and dedicated substitute parent and grandparent to me and my kids for almost twenty years. Thank you!

Foreword

"The word is near you; it is in your mouth and in your heart," that is, the word of faith we are proclaiming: That if you confess with your mouth, "Jesus is Lord," and believe in your heart that God raised him from the dead, you will be saved. For it is with your heart that you believe and are justified, and it is with your mouth that you confess and are saved. As the Scripture says, "Anyone who trusts in him will never be put to shame."

Romans 10:8-11

I must admit that my book is primarily for Christian parents and children. However, if anyone is not a Christian, then it is simply a matter of doing as the above Scripture directs. One must have faith that Jesus exists and then confess with the mouth that He is Lord. Upon believing that God raised Jesus from the dead, one will be saved. If we will admit that we are sinners and need Him, all of heaven will celebrate as we become heirs of everything God has to offer us through His Word, the Bible.

At least one-third of this book is Scripture; that is because it is important to live according to the way that God has instructed us. Some things in the Word may seem incredulous to a Christian, let alone a non-Christian, but we must have faith and know that if He said it, He will back it up.

There are so many ways we can pass on a blessing to our children. One way is with the words that proceed from our mouths. With our words, we can build our children up, or we can tear them down. Being good responsible parents is not an easy job, and it is not for the weak. It is not good to let children have their way and do what they want at any time. It takes a lot of praying and studying what God's Word says about our relationships with kids, spouses, and people in general. I include spouses and other people because our children are affected not only by the way we treat them but also by the way they see us treat our spouses and other people.

It is important to include the Creator in raising our children. He is their Creator too, and He knows them best. No matter the circumstances, He has a plan for their lives. They are not here on this earth just to be our offspring and carry out our wishes.

The Scriptures used in this book emphasize the importance of what the Bible says about the way we treat our kids and the words we speak to them. These Scriptures can be looked up in the various translations. It is important for us to pray over our children, love them unconditionally, respect them, protect them, discipline them while not provoking them to anger, spend time with them, and teach them to love and care for others. We must teach them about life situations, money matters and credit, truthfulness, self-control, hanging around good people, and making a stand for what is good and true. They simply must be taught to forgive, because forgiveness will free their spirits. Unforgiveness, on the other hand, hurts the person holding on to the bitterness more than it does the person it is directed towards, and this is a proven fact. Most of all, we must remember that our children will learn by the example we set before them in our actions, reactions, and lack of actions. We dare not be negligent in the stewardship we have been given over our children.

In this book, I do share some of my experiences and mistakes I have made with my kids for all to know and learn from. Among parents that have made mistakes, I am one of the chief. In my desire to love and protect my children, I have sometimes been a dictator. "Because I said so" can't be the answer all the time.

You may or may not have made the same mistakes I made, but there are many varieties of ways to miss the mark. However, Jesus is present to help us all. He has helped and is helping me, and He will help you too.

Not everybody is loveable, and this applies to both parents and children. Unforgiveness can affect us in negative ways mentally, physically, spiritually, emotionally, and socially. I'm sure it can harm us in even more ways than I have mentioned.

I pray that this book will not be a discouragement to you in areas where you are weak or have erred. It may hurt initially to face the truth, but joy will come in the newness of your relationship with your children. It is my desire to shine a light on the shortcomings of us all, for the sake of our children, their children, and the generations to come. We can make things right for our future grandchildren and great-grandchildren.

Although there is much talk about not wanting things to be passed down to our children and grandchildren, many people still aren't living the example of loving others. But we can stop behaviors that are not good from being passed along—they can stop with us. Let's pass the blessings of a good example in both word and deed to the next generation!

Table of Content

Part 1 15

Example to our Children 17

Respect/Honor 53

Discipline/Tough Love 62

Protect/Guard 71

The Gift of Children 79

Provoke not to Anger 87

Their Gift- not our Dream 92

Bad Company 98

Responsible for Actions 104

Don't awake Love 113

Men are Needed 124

A Good Mother 134

Intercession – Build a Wall or Hedge around them 141

Spoken Word 150

When Bad seems Good 159

Forsaken – Parents out of Life 165

Spending Time 170

Self-Control..179

Make a Stand/Take a stand 188

Lies/Truth...194

Good Stewart of Money..209

Failure to Plan is a Plan to Fail 228

Prayer 239

Forgive / Let it go 250

Loving God/ Loving One Another..262

Part 2..**291**

Carrie's Child...295

Part 3..**303**

Pass the Blessings, Please!

(The poem)..307

May the words of my mouth and the meditation of my heart be pleasing in your sight, O LORD, my Rock and my Redeemer.

Psalms 19:14

Part 1

EXAMPLE
(Ready, Set, Go)

Getting ready means we are making up our minds and accepting the call to be the parents God has called us to be to our children and other youth, which really are our future.

To set our minds means we're making deliberate steps and many efforts to insure success in our plan to be good parents.

Getting ready and setting our minds is the prerequisite before we go and put actions to the plan. To go is important because our kids won't know if we have made up our minds to get ready and get set to help them. The action word go will be evidence to them that we truly care for them and love them.

Generally, for better or worse, children imitate their parents or other adults in their lives. Unfortunately, sometimes children do this without even realizing what they are doing. That's because we all tend to do what has been done to us.

Like a seed, we reproduce after our own kind. When we allow children to see certain behavior consistently, then that is the behavior that will probably become theirs. They need, therefore, to see us choosing high standards to live by and know that they, too, are expected to live by these standards. The standard, of course, must be within their reach and not something that is always just beyond what they can grab. It has to be attainable to a certain extent for them not to lose hope and become discouraged in continuing to try their best. All children are not the same, and a child should not be expected to attain something that another sibling or another child has attained. We should make each of them feel special in their talents.

Jesus made Himself a living example for us.

Then God said, "Let us make man in our image, in our likeness,… So God created man in his own image, in the image of God he created him; male and female he created them.

Genesis 1:26-27

We are to be in God's image, not in someone else's. God has a plan for each of our children's lives, and it may not be the lives or professions we envision for them. They possess natural God-given abilities for the gift or gifts that God has placed inside of them. But there is something about us parents that makes us want to see little look-alikes of ourselves running around.

We can ruin our relationship with our kids by pushing them in directions they are not bent towards. How sad it is to try to make a square peg fit into a round hole!

Some part of it will surely be damaged if we force it into a place it was never meant to be. When God said, "Let us make man in our own image," this was and is a good thing. We are meant to reflect the image of God that He has desired for us since the beginning of time. Some people were meant to go to college, and some were not. There is nothing wrong with having a trade. Not everyone will be an A student in everything. We should, therefore, pray to God and observe our children's interests. We need discernment so that we don't interfere with God's desires for their lives. We should place value on our relationship with our children and listen to their hearts.

To our children, we are to be examples of lives lived for Christ. It matters what we do privately just as much as what we do publicly. The private and public lives need to match. We can't scream and mistreat our children at home and then expect them to tell everyone that we are the best parents in the world. It is not easy to live this type of consistent life, because sometimes it hurts. However, for the sake of our children, it is necessary.

To this you were called, because Christ suffered for you, leaving you an example, that you should follow in his steps. –

1 Peter 2:21

Sometimes it is hard to set a good example for our children, but if we just think of the impressionable eyes that are not only watching us but also copying us, then we can find the strength to curtail some behaviors. Our children may also learn bad behavior by watching certain TV programs and reading certain books. As parents, we should know Christ, teach Christ, and live Christ.

Jesus gave us visual examples of how we should treat others.

When He had finished washing their feet, He put on his clothes and returned to His place." Do you understand what I have done for you?' He asked them. "You call me Teacher and Lord," and rightly so for that is what I am. Now that I, your Lord and Teacher, have washed your feet, you also should wash one another's feet. I have set you an example that you should do as I have done for you

John 13:12-15

I wish I could say that I have always been a good example for my children all of their lives. But I have screamed and acted ugly with my children on many occasions, both at home and in public. In my insanity, I thought I was supposed to dominate them. I thought I was always right, and I thought they were wrong if they did not agree with me in my wrongness. I didn't let them speak up or speak out because none of those things had been allowed in my childhood.

God knew that I needed a husband like the one that I have. He was not raised the way I was, and the mistreatment that my kids received from my mouth did not sit well with him. I was embarrassed when he caught me acting and reacting with my kids in a less than desirable manner. I had always wanted to be a good mother to my children; the desire had been there from the beginning. Although I wasn't quite sure how the parent that I wanted to be should behave, I knew I was not doing it right. On the other hand, I noticed my husband's patience and kindness with our children. I watched the way he listened to them and stood there eye to eye with them. I could see this made them feel valued.

Our children will imitate the good they see in us, if it is there to be found. However, they will also imitate the bad in us, if it is there to be found. Let's get ourselves together, for their sake! Some people may not be as bad as I was in the area of my weakness, but there are many ways to err. Some people are too soft and lenient and won't discipline their kids. This can be just as detrimental as being too harsh because kids do need discipline. It is not good for kids to be allowed to talk back, because if they aren't respectful to their parents, they will not be respectful to other adults. Furthermore, if they see awful examples in the way we treat our parents, then there is a chance they will repeat the behavior. Why gamble? But most important of all, if children are not taught proper respect, they will not learn to be respectful to God in His commands.

Our children are born with the ability to do the things that we do. God can and will provide them with the ability to not follow in the ways of their parent and grandparents. Especially when they are older and realize something their parents do may not be what God would have them do. God wants us to come to Him and ask for help from generational bondages. It is not inborn in us that we must follow in our parent's footstep. However, we will probably imitate the behavior that we see and what we hear. Most times prejudice parents will probably have prejudice kids. Abusive parents will probably have abusive kids. Alcoholic parents will probably have alcoholic kids. Welfare and teenage parents will probably have welfare and teenage kids. Parents with bad attitudes will probably have kids with bad attitudes. Parents that are not respectful of authority will probably have kids that have a problem with authority. Parents that went to college will probably have kids that will go to college. Church-going parents will probably have church-going kids. Hard working parents will probably have hard working kids. I'm not saying that this is the rule but generally it happens. We don't have to follow in their steps but we do tend to do the things that we see. Let's look at some biblical examples of this. Let's start with David and follow his generations for a while.

David was a man of God and this was the most prominent thing that he passed to his generations that followed behind him.

David also had issues with women. He loved having beautiful women. According to II Samuel 3:2-5, he had six wives. In II Samuel 6:16, he had a wife by the name of Michal. In I Chronicles 14-3, he added more wives in Jerusalem. There were thirteen children born in Jerusalem. We don't know how many of these children had the same mother. However, there were many wives. Even in I Kings 1:3, they searched for a beautiful woman and brought her to the king but he was not intimate with her. They knew then that he was very sick.

Solomon was king after David. He served God as his father, David before him had. When God came to Solomon and asked what he could give to him. Solomon responded that he wanted wisdom to rule the great multitude of God's people. God granted his wish and made him very wealthy.

God said to Solomon, "Since this is your heart's desire and you have not asked for wealth, riches or honor, nor for the death of your enemies, and since you have not asked for a long life but for wisdom and knowledge to govern my people over whom I have made you king, therefore wisdom and knowledge will be given you. And I will also give you wealth, riches and honor, such as no king who was before you ever had and none after you will have."

2 Chronicles 1:11-12

Solomon was a very wise man and therefore it would stand to reason that some of his children would be wise, also. He was often in the palace dispersing judgment to the people. I'm sure that his sons had to be amazed with their father's wisdom.

Solomon loved women also just as his father David. He desired many wives. Let's go back to see why this was wrong.

Be sure to appoint over you the king the Lord your God chooses. He must be from among your own brothers. Do not place a foreigner over you, one who is not a brother Israelite. The king, moreover, must not acquire great numbers of horses for himself or make the people return to Egypt to get more of them, for the Lord has told you," You are not to go back that way again." He must not take many wives, or his heart will be led astray. He must not accumulate large amounts of silver and gold.

Deuteronomy 17:15-17

God had made it plain that they were not to have many wives. The very thing that he said would happen to David and Solomon and other kings, happened. Sin has a way of progressing to the next stage. It spreads and defiles with each generation. David did have many wives but they were from his own people even though Solomon's mother was first the wife of Uriah, whom David had killed. David was repentant and asked for forgiveness from God.

Let's look at the things that Solomon did after all that God had blessed him with.

Even though he did acquire many horses when God had said not to do so, it was the many wives that caused the downfall of Solomon. Let's read

"'King Solomon, however, loved many foreign women besides Pharaoh's daughter — Moabites, Ammonites, Edomites, Sidonians and Hittites. They were from nations about which the LORD had told the Israelites, "You must not intermarry with them, because they will surely turn your hearts after their gods." Nevertheless, Solomon held fast to them in love. He had seven hundred wives of royal birth and three hundred concubines, and his wives led him astray. As Solomon grew old, his wives turned his heart after other gods, and his heart was not fully devoted to the LORD his God, as the heart of David his father had been. He followed Ashtoreth the goddess of the Sidonians, and Molech the detestable god of the Ammonites. So Solomon did evil in the eyes of the LORD; he did not follow the LORD completely, as David his father had done.'"

1 Kings 11:1-8

Ashtoreth was the Canaanite goddess of fertility whose worship involved sexual rites and astrology. The worship of another wife included human sacrifices, including children. Another was equally cruel and also was involved in astrology. These women were obviously not worshipers of the God of David or Solomon. David had more wives than he was supposed to but his sons took it to a whole new level. Solomon not only had an excessive number of wives but they were not women that he should have been involved with. Now Rehoboam, the son of

Solomon took several wives but not as many as his father and grandfather, never the less he did take more than one.

Rehoboam loved Maacah daughter of Absalom more than any of his other wives and concubines. In all, he had eighteen wives and sixty concubines, twenty-eight sons and sixty daughters.

2 Chronicles 11:2

All the rest of the kings did the same thing one after the other. The bible continually says, "they followed in the steps of their fathers before them". Some followed for good and some not. You see we have a choice in how we live our lives.

Now fear the LORD and serve him with all faithfulness. Throw away the gods your forefathers worshiped beyond the River and in Egypt, and serve the LORD. But if serving the LORD seems undesirable to you, then choose for yourselves this day whom you will serve, whether the gods your forefathers served beyond the River, or the gods of the Amorites, in whose land you are living. But as for me and my household, we will serve the LORD.

Joshua 24:14-15

Rehoboam also did evil in the sight of the Lord like Solomon did in his life by forsaking the Lord. So on down the lineage of David, some were disobedience, worshiping other gods, the temple was built and the things of God were established and some tore the sacred things down. To the extreme that some desecrated God's word, others were at the other end in their zeal to obey. It was all a matter of choice even though things were made common by the way their fathers before them lived.

There are times when it is not our direct behavior that is a bad influence to our children but the people and places we expose them to in our lives. Lot was a good example of making things common to his daughters by living in a horrible place. He didn't show value to them either as the story went along.

Lot looked up and saw that the whole plain of the Jordan was well watered, like the garden of the LORD, like the land of Egypt, toward Zoar. (This was before the LORD destroyed Sodom and Gomorrah.)So Lot chose for himself the whole plain of the Jordan and set out toward the east. The two men parted company: Abram lived in the land of Canaan, while Lot lived among the cities of the plain and pitched his tents near Sodom. Now the men of Sodom were wicked and were sinning greatly against the LORD.

Genesis 13:10-13

Sometimes when we see what we think to be a great neighborhood to live in, we need to do our research and ask God for His opinion. The people there may be bad influences on you and your family. It may have lush lawns that are well-kept and beautiful houses that are immaculate. But what are the people in the neighborhood like. Are they unfriendly, prejudice, meddlesome, living beyond their means, unruly kids that the parents let them run wild and they make excuses for them and so on and so on? The kids are having wild parties and they won't have to go far for the alcohol and prescription drugs because plenty can be found in their parent's cabinet. Teenage girls may get pregnant but the parent can afford an abortion. It may seem like it may be a good place to live in outward appearance but not such a good place to live for your family. These people will influence your family if you are not careful. Your kids will have to go to school with them and there will probably be pressures to have what they have and do what they do.

They could also live in a housing project or other low rent place that some of the people don't take care for their homes. In many cases, there will be one parent living in each home. Most people will live on some type of government assistance. This may mean that many won't have jobs. Many of the teenage girls may have babies and won't finish school. The guys may have dropped out of school and fathered several kids. Many of them won't finish high school either. A good percentage won't attend college. Unfortunately, several may have a visit with the judicial system. Where are their dreams?! I'm not saying this is the case for every set of government homes. Some choose this way of life because that's the way their mother and grandmother and great- grandmother lived this way and some see it as an inexpensive and carefree life. My question is, "Is it worth it?" Both kids, in the well to do neighborhood and the not doing so well neighborhood, are victims of their parent's lifestyle and both are suffering.

The LORD has made the Jordan a boundary between us and you—you Reubenites and Gadites! You have no share in the LORD.' So your descendants might cause ours to stop fearing the LORD.

Joshua 22:25

We have to make every effort to guard out families from the assaults of the evil one. Get rid of anything that set itself before God. We have to separate our families as much as we can from things that would make them sympathetic to ways that are not of God. We will be shown what is not good for our families in our homes. Some examples are reading of horoscopes (some people can't start their day unless they have read their horoscope), some have to go and get their palms read by sister Mary or someone like this, some have to burn money candles in belief that this will bring them money and good fortune, some have Buddha's in their homes as decoration, we allow our kids to play with Ouija boards, Tara cards, dungeons and dragons, some allow their kids to play all source of evil and vile video games, some allow the kids to be on the computer in private places in the home (this media can be used for good and bad and there are predators out there), reading popular witchcraft books that are meant to draw your kids in or at the very least, make them sympathetic to the various ungodly works, watching horrible videos on TV and at the movies with violence, sexual scenes, and language that is vulgar or making them again sympathetic to causes that are clearly not a part of what God says, listening to vulgar things on the radio, repeating things from all the medias that they don't know what they are saying and agreeing to, doing séances for fun, etc. We have to drive these things out of our homes. There is no such thing as they are just having childish fun or it is harmless. They may be children but it is not harmless.

Then the men of Judah went with the Simeonites their brothers and attacked the Canaanites living in Zephath, and they totally destroyed the city. Therefore it was called Hormah.

The Benjamites, however, failed to dislodge the Jebusites, who were living in Jerusalem; to this day the Jebusites live there with the Benjamites.

But Manasseh did not drive out the people of Beth Shan or Taanach or Dor or Ibleam or Megiddo and their surrounding settlements, for the Canaanites were determined to live in that land. When Israel became strong, they pressed the Canaanites into forced labor but never drove them out completely. Nor did Ephraim drive out the Canaanites living in Gezer, but the Canaanites continued to live there among them.

Pass the Blessings!

Neither did Zebulun drive out the Canaanites living in Kitron or Nahalol, who remained among them; but they did subject them to forced labor. Nor did Asher drive out those living in Acco or Sidon or Ahlab or Aczib or Helbah or Aphek or Rehob, and because of this the people of Asher lived among the Canaanite inhabitants of the land. Neither did Naphtali drive out those living in Beth Shemesh or Beth Anath; but the Naphtalites too lived among the Canaanite inhabitants of the land, and those living in Beth Shemesh and Beth Anath became forced laborers for them.

The angel of the LORD went up from Gilgal to Bokim and said, "I brought you up out of Egypt and led you into the land that I swore to give to your forefathers. I said, 'I will never break my covenant with you, 2and you shall not make a covenant with the people of this land, but you shall break down their altars.' Yet you have disobeyed me. Why have you done this? 3Now therefore I tell you that I will not drive them out before you; they will be thorns in your sides and their gods will be a snare to you."

Judges 1:17, 21,27-33, Judges 2:1-3

We must be diligent in taking our home back from the enemy. We know that God wants this done and we must do it completely. If not, they will have the opportunity to rub off on our families and us.

As in the case of Lot, he chose the seemingly better place than Abraham but in the long run, it was nothing but trouble for him. The people there were without morals or had no regard for God. We can't worry about people calling us intolerant of others because if God says certain behavior is wrong, then IT IS WRONG! If we don't do as the Lord says and bring down idols totally, our children will wrestle with the same strongholds. The common, everyday habits of ours will become theirs unless they see other Godly examples. I really feel sorry for kids born to some actors and actresses, some politicians and other government officials and even some preacher kids and other jobs. Unless, the parents take drastic and on-purpose measures to protect their kids from the issues and influences of their jobs, then it may turn out to be devastating to the children. Just because the parent has the ability to give the child everything they want, does not mean the child should get everything they want. I have an idea! Take them shopping to make purchases for others. We are blessed to be a blessing!

At this time Amraphel king of Shinar, Arioch king of Ellasar, Kedorlaomer king of Elam and Tidal king of Goiim went to war against Bera king of Sodom, Birsha king of Gomorrah, Shinab king of Admah, Shemeber king of Zeboiim, and the king of Bela (that is, Zoar).

The four kings seized all the goods of Sodom and Gomorrah and all their food; then they went away. They also carried off Abram's nephew Lot and his possessions, since he was living in Sodom.

During the night Abram divided his men to attack them and he routed them, pursuing them as far as Hobah, north of Damascus. He recovered all the goods and brought back his relative Lot and his possessions, together with the women and the other people.

Genesis 14:1-2, 11-12,15-16

First of all, it seems that Lot was trouble for Abram. First, he tries to pick out the best land for himself, when God had in reality given all the land of Abram. Then he stays with a detestable people with horrible morals.

Later, Abram has to rescue him from the trouble that he was in because he lived in this place. But to make matters worse, can you believe that he moved back there after Abram rescued him the first time? If we were to rewind the tape, God did not tell Abram to bring Lot with him on this trip. Some of the problems in our lives are there because we are doing things contrary to what we were directed to do from God. Some people are in our lives and they should not be because of the problems and issues they stir up.

Let's read a good bit of Genesis 19. This is a very interesting story that you will learn a great deal from Lot, who was Abram's cousin.

The two angels arrived at Sodom in the evening, and Lot was sitting in the gateway of the city. When he saw them, he got up to meet them and bowed down with his face to the ground. "My lords," he said, "please turn aside to your servant's house. You can wash your feet and spend the night and then go on your way early in the morning."

"No," they answered, "we will spend the night in the square."

But he insisted so strongly that they did go with him and entered his house. He prepared a meal for them, baking bread without yeast, and they ate. Before they had gone to bed, all the men from every part of the city of Sodom—both young and old—surrounded the house. They called to Lot, "Where are the men who came to you tonight? Bring them out to us so that we can have sex with them."

Lot went outside to meet them and shut the door behind him and said, "No, my friends. Don't do this wicked thing. Look, I have two daughters who have never slept with a man. Let me bring them out to you, and you can do what you like with them. But don't do anything to these men, for they have come under the protection of my roof."

"Get out of our way," they replied. And they said, "This fellow came here as an alien, and now he wants to play the judge! We'll treat you worse than them." They kept bringing pressure on Lot and moved forward to break down the door.

But the men inside reached out and pulled Lot back into the house and shut the door. Then they struck the men who were at the door of the house, young and old, with blindness so that they could not find the door.

The two men said to Lot, "Do you have anyone else here—sons-in-law, sons or daughters, or anyone else in the city who belongs to you? Get them out of here, because we are going to destroy this place. The outcry to the LORD against its people is so great that he has sent us to destroy it."

So Lot went out and spoke to his sons-in-law, who were pledged to marry his daughters. He said, "Hurry and get out of this place, because the LORD is about to destroy the city!" But his sons-in-law thought he was joking.

With the coming of dawn, the angels urged Lot, saying, "Hurry! Take your wife and your two daughters who are here, or you will be swept away when the city is punished."

When he hesitated, the men grasped his hand and the hands of his wife and of his two daughters and led them safely out of the city, for the LORD was merciful to them. As soon as they had brought them out, one of them said, "Flee for your lives! Don't look back, and don't stop anywhere in the plain! Flee to the mountains or you will be swept away!"

But Lot said to them, "No, my lords, please! Your servant has found favor in your eyes, and you have shown great kindness to me in sparing my life. But I can't flee to the mountains; this disaster will overtake me, and I'll die. Look, here is a town near enough to run to, and it is small. Let me flee to it—it is very small, isn't it? Then my life will be spared."

He said to him, "Very well, I will grant this request too; I will not overthrow the town you speak of. But flee there quickly, because I cannot do anything until you reach it." (That is why the town was called Zoar.)

By the time Lot reached Zoar, the sun had risen over the land. Then the LORD rained down burning sulfur on Sodom and Gomorrah—from the LORD out of the heavens. Thus he overthrew those cities and the entire plain, including all those living in the cities—and also the vegetation in the land. But Lot's wife looked back, and she became a pillar of salt.

Lot and his two daughters left Zoar and settled in the mountains, for he was afraid to stay in Zoar. He and his two daughters lived in a cave. One day the older daughter said to the younger, "Our father is old, and there is no man around here to lie with us, as is the custom all over the earth. Let's get our father to drink wine and then lie with him and preserve our family line through our father."

That night they got their father to drink wine, and the older daughter went in and lay with him. He was not aware of it when she lay down or when she got up.

The next day the older daughter said to the younger, "Last night I lay with my father. Let's get him to drink wine again tonight, and you go in and lie with him so we can preserve our family line through our father." So they got their father to drink wine that night also, and the younger daughter went and lay with him. Again he was not aware of it when she lay down or when she got up.

So both of Lot's daughters became pregnant by their father.

Genesis 19:1-24, 26, 30-36

First of all, he made a bad choice in staying with those immoral people. Those people had no shame at all in their lifestyles. It was not only himself that Lot was exposing to this atmosphere. His wife and daughters were being influenced. Lot offered his virgin daughters to the men of the city but they wanted to be with the men. I wonder how Lot's daughters felt after being offered up like that. Lot had to be convinced to leave the city for he had great possessions there. We know he was doing well financially because his home was located near the gate where the elders and the wealthy stayed. At what price did his success come? How did his family hold up spiritually? Did Lot's family know of the God of Abraham? I often wonder why he was so drawn to the place. We know that the only reason that he and his family were spared was because of Abraham. Thank God for praying family and friends. Sometimes, people and places are spared because of praying people. It is ultimately what He knows is best. In some cases, the sins of a place or family are great and we do have free will.

When he did leave the city, his wife looked back; obviously she was very attached to something that was back there. Could it be possessions or the city's fast life style?

A lot of people are drawn to the fast life to their destruction. Why did Lot's wife look back? Who knows, but what wasn't on her mind was her family, getting away from that place and obeying the instructions of the two men. Her family suffered for her mistake. The life that her daughters had been exposed to became evident. The girls lived in a place where the choices for a spouse or even a male friend were few. The options weren't there since they didn't know God and therefore could not trust that He would provide. The husband-to-be would not even leave the city after their soon-to-be father-in-law had warned them. The girl's heart and naïve thoughts may have been in the right place but they went about it in the wrong manner. When we make depravity common to our children, then why are we surprised at their choices? The heart may be in the right place but the actions were not. We can have God given desires and actions but achieve them in the wrong way. Being hungry at an extreme can become gluttony. Being alone, and not wanting to be, can become illicit relationships. Providing for our family can become greedy and covetousness, if we don't keep in mind the things that God wants for our family. Being cautious can become over protective and overbearing, and not trusting God.

Lot's daughters were intimate with their father. They thought their father was the only man left on earth. They became pregnant by him. It seems that Lot didn't teach them about Abraham and the Lord God. They became what he made common to them. IMMORAL women! I'm not saying that they didn't have a choice. They did. However, this is the environment the young ladies were raised.

Assemble the people—men, women and children, and the aliens living in your towns—so they can listen and learn to fear the LORD your God and follow carefully all the words of this law. Their children, who do not know this law, must hear it and learn to fear the LORD your God as long as you live in the land you are crossing the Jordan to possess."

Deuteronomy 31:12-13

We have to make every effort to make sure that our families are in healthy, godly environments. Unless they find out about God, they will probably become like the people that are around them.

Above all else, guard your heart, for it is the wellspring of life.

Proverbs 4:23

Our children see so much corruption on the television. While my kids were growing up, there were five TVs in my home. They saw so much cartoon violence and bad harsh kidding between kids. They saw sibling being harsh to each other, talking back to their parents and smarting off and just being plain disobedient. I have to admit that some of this also comes from their parents. I don't like those shows but I watched them because I was interested in what was being deposited into my children. I was also strict about what movies they watch at home and at the theater. In the early years, I was careful with the video games they play, books they read, friends they choose, and people that I let them hang around with. At a certain point, I had to back off and let them make their decision. It does cause conflict but I was supposed to watch out for my children. I was careful about what enters their heads and their ears because it affects their hearts. All of these collective things will form their opinions and choices throughout their life. Even then we have to continually stay before the Lord and pray without ceasing for the help to be what each other needs. If we don't, then we will not reap the blessing of a godly home. It will be a family thing of doing wrong. The whole family tends to get involved with disobeying God. Then we start shying away from church and reading the word, thus our decline.

Do you not see what they are doing in the towns of Judah and in the streets of Jerusalem? [1]The children gather wood, the fathers light the fire, and the women knead the dough and make cakes of bread for the Queen of Heaven. They pour out drink offerings to other gods to provoke me to anger.

Jeremiah 7:17-18

Doing wrong was a family affair. Everyone had his or her part to play and are guilty of sin. God was indeed angry with them. It can also affect the family in physical and tangible ways if the parents aren't serving God and/or something happens to them because of their actions. Here's another example.

May his children be fatherless and his wife a widow. May his children be wandering beggars; may they be driven from their ruined homes. May a creditor seize all he has; may strangers plunder the fruits of his labor. May no one extend kindness to him or take pity on his fatherless children. May his descendants be cut off, their names blotted out from the next generation. May the iniquity of his fathers be remembered before the LORD; may the sin of his mother never be blotted out.

Psalms 109:9-14

The parent did something wrong and the children are suffering because of it. The creditor will take what they own because of none payment. The children are left homeless and begging for bread and will probably end up in foster care and/or the welfare system. Unless things improve for these children, they may end up on the street and killed (thus his posterity or next generation is being cut off).

Rid yourselves of all the offenses you have committed, and get a new heart and a new spirit. Why will you die, O house of Israel? 32For I take no pleasure in the death of anyone, declares the Sovereign LORD. Repent and live!

Ezekiel 18:31-32

God really does want the best for us. He made us in His good pleasure. He knew what we were and are capable of and yet He loves us and wants the best for us.

What we do can have a definite affect on our families. However, we can also do things that affect our children in a positive way. Take Noah and his family for instance.

But I will establish my covenant with you, and you will enter the ark—you and your sons and your wife and your sons' wives with you.

Genesis 6:18

God is making the covenant with Noah but He is allowing the wife, sons and their wives to come along with him. There are kids that aren't being blessed because of their parents. We can turn all of this around and do well and be a good influence to our families. We can teach our children the Ten Commandments, not just moral things because that is a matter of opinion. We need to actively teach them the things of God. We need to be proactive and then we won't have to be reactive. Being reactive means it has already happened and you try and make it right, proactive is to live a life that is a good example and teach our children why we do what we do and why we believe the way we believe.

Be imitators of God, therefore, as dearly loved children and live a life of love, just as Christ loved us and gave himself up for us as a fragrant offering and sacrifice to God.

Ephesians 5:1-2

God wants us to imitate Him just as our children will imitate us. Christ was an example to us of his own free will and it was not without a price. Our being an example to our children should be the same way. Sacrificial!!! When we make the decision to become parents, we must be willing to give ourselves as an offering and as a sacrifice. Society says - when is it my turn to be me or when do I do the things that I want to? We should not let society decide or be our moral compass. God has set a standard for us to live. Women's lib did a lot of damage to the family. It is true, women should be paid the same pay for equal work but the other things that got attached to that really hurt our families.

One more thing the above scripture talks about is for us to walk in love. Walk is an action word. We need to show them love by our actions. By living our lives as true examples of what God would have us to be and do. If kids are seeing us in bad relationships, cheating and scheming, driving too fast, constantly shopping, being prejudice, lying, etc.

…What do we expect them to do with this information? Surely, we don't say – do as I say do, not as I do. We will stand before God for being double-minded.

The righteous man leads a blameless life; blessed are his children after him.

Proverbs 20:7

How many things do we make common with our children? How many things should their little minds gasp at but they don't because they are familiar with things that they shouldn't be. No, I'm not saying that we should keep them locked up. They can know about things without seeing them and seeing them and seeing them. Think back 40 to 50 years ago, when teenage pregnancies were less common and taboo. When boys felt they had some responsibility in this and would at least attempt to marry the girl. Husbands and wives give up so quickly on their marriages. Kids see Dad hitting on Mom and Mom hitting on Dad. They see and experience so much verbal and physical abuse between their parents. Most will repeat the things they see in their homes. I often sit and wonder what behaviors my kids will imitate from my husband and myself. Will it be the silent treatments or the teasing of each other or the way my husband takes care of the family or the way Mom tried to be around for them or the fussing Mom always did or the overprotection of them or the way Dad would listen patiently to whatever they wanted to talk about (as long as it wasn't during one of his shows, thank you to the person that invented TiVo). How will it affect them when I pushed them so hard in school work and in chores and in discipline? I often try to explain to them why I do the things I do. Will they understand? Will they know that I meant them well? I wish they came with manuals. I wish I knew what wouldn't work before I ever tried it or a least how it would affect each individual child. I can't even repeat what I do for one that would not be good to do with the other. They are so different individually.

My mother was a single parent and she had to work hard. She was also in a relationship that took her away from the house often. I remember wanting to spend time with her but I couldn't. There were so many of us and so little time. I remember the hurting feeling that I felt and I started to withdraw. This was the only way that I could protect myself was to decide that I didn't need people and didn't want them touching me. I remember the man that my mother was involved with was abusive to her. That was where it stopped because she didn't let him abuse us at all. When I was in my first marriage, my ex was abusive physically, mentally, verbally, sexually, emotionally and spiritually. I thought this was all right because I had observed this behavior. Another sibling allowed this also in their marriage. I saw an uncle behaving this way. I wouldn't have thought that I would have tolerated this behavior but there I was and I hated the predicament.

(It is o.k. to let our kids know that they can surpass us in life. However, if they see it, there is a greater possibility that they will repeat it or at the very least, tolerate it).

My intensity to be a good parent would drive me to almost a breaking point at times.

It is a bit of a struggle for me to just be content with being a wife and mother. I love my husband!!! However, it was my desire to teach my children the right way to live and for them to be productive people of this world, which seem to drive me and them to a breaking point at times. I would do anything for them, even to death. However, I must confess that there is a flight spirit within me. I want to just runaway sometimes. I hate that so much. When things got really hard, I would get in my car and drive and cry and talk to God. I wanted His help for guidance in my failing plan as it seemed to me. It seemed like I was always failing at my goals. I remember on one occasion, I felt His hand on my head and He said he had a plan for me and He was going to use me through all of the pain of myself and my family to help others.

He who is full loathes honey, but to the hungry even what is bitter tastes sweet.

Proverbs 27:7

A child that has received well is not easily turned to the side because someone else being nice to them. Whether it is gangs, cults and/or controlling-abusive relationships, they won't be deceived. However, if they haven't received the affirmation and love at home, then anything is sweet. Any attention, any words, any closeness will be taken as good even though it is bitter. Take for instance a sponge, a dry sponge will take in anything, but a fully soaked sponge is full and is less likely to take in anything. As I sit and write, I am so convicted with my own children. I need to fill them more with my love and the love of God.

When I was growing up, I lived in a housing project. I know the intent may have been done with good intention but these places can do harm to a child's future. I'm all for the idea of people being able to find an affordable place to live, but these places can be a breeding ground for 'no-dreams' for many kids and adults. You see, I thought it was normal to have little. I thought it was normal to not get married but have kids anyway. I thought it was normal to have a child as a teenager. I didn't see my options for many of the careers that interested me. (As an adult, I would love to have been a doctor and a Geneticist to be more specific. This generational thing is so intriguing to me. I watch and listen to everything I can on DNA, genome and the whole epigenome project. I would like to know how we pass things to our children not only physically, mentally, emotionally, socially, financially and spiritually but by the everyday choices we make and are exposed to. All of our decisions have the potential to affect our generations. We can't say it's my life and I'll live it the way that I want to because my decisions affect only me. This simply is not true! I thought it was normal not to have a car. I thought it was normal to have a tooth ache and just pay $12.00 to get it taken out of your mouth. (Later on in life, I had a good job with good insurance. I was having problems with a tooth. I went to the dentist and asked him to extract it. He asked me, 'Why did I want him to do that?' I didn't know any other way existed to take care of the problem. He introduced me to the world of cleanings, root canal and fillings. He saved my tooth in spite of my ignorance.)

I did see my mother trying hard to get off public assistance and out of public housing. She did domestic work and she worked in the shoe department at JCPenney. They made her a buyer in the children's department. It didn't last long, because they soon took it from her because she didn't have a degree or the experience in that area and others complaining in jealousy. I felt they would have come up with a reason no matter what she did. That little time at that position was such an inspiration to me. My dry sponge soaked that in and I felt hope enter my life. I watched as my mother went through many other difficulties. Even the church would ostracize her. She went through these things on her knees. Life kept trying to knock her down but she didn't let it. Tough times don't last but tough peoples do. Thanks Mom!

There was an incident that happened when I was in my mid-thirties. I couldn't believe it! An unspeakable thing was happening! Do we do things like that? Do we allow this to go on in our family? These were my questions. The decision was being made to put my grandfather in a nursing home. It was hard for me to believe. I was scared for this to happen. True, I didn't know all the reasons why this decision was made. I just know that it was hurtful. If this door was opened once, what would stop it from being opened again? Now that it has been done, where does it stop? Will I think that it is o.k. now that it has been done to granddaddy? It was repeated again in our family but I wasn't as awestruck as I was with my grandfather. Please understand, I know sometimes there is just no other choice but should they be almost forgotten or visited maybe once a week or less. They are still our relatives, they still have feeling and they still hurt. They also will need for us to stand up for them and protect them in some of these institutions.

But from everlasting to everlasting the LORD's love is with those who fear him, and his righteousness with their children's children— with those who keep his covenant and remember to obey his precepts.

Psalms 103:17-18

Even our children' children can benefits from the home of a godly family.

All the men of Judah, with their wives and children and little ones, stood there before the LORD.

2 Chronicles 20:13

A good man leaves an inheritance for his children's children,...

Proverbs 13:22

We need to leave an inheritance of godly living to our children. We need to worship before the Lord together as a family. It is not too late for us to establish godly rules and relationships with our children and husband or wife. However, it's imperative that we do so because there is a definite attack on the family. The enemy is working to destroy the family between man, woman and children. In so doing, the world is being destroyed. When people don't care about others, animals and the environment, which are God's creation, then how can they possibly care about the creator? If we call on His name and make the necessary changes in our families, then he will heal our land.

If my people, who are called by my name, will humble themselves and pray and seek my face and turn from their wicked ways, then will I hear from heaven and will forgive their sin and will heal their land.

2 Chronicles 7:14

All we have to do is realize that we are doing it wrong and ask for his help. We can't do it on our own. That's all we need to do.

May the LORD make you increase, both you and your children.

Psalms 115:14

Would God rather have our children at church just for presence? Would He rather want their money or good works? I don't believe so.

Pass the Blessings!

But Samuel replied: "Does the LORD delight in burnt offerings and sacrifices as much as in obeying the voice of the LORD? To obey is better than sacrifice, and to heed is better than the fat of rams. For rebellion is like the sin of divination, and arrogance like the evil of idolatry. Because you have rejected the word of the LORD,

1 Samuel 15:22-23

God would rather have our obedience and loyalties to Him, than our money, going to church, doing good works and other things that we do in trying to obey God. Where our treasure is there will our heart be also. Rebellion and insubordination is our desire to do our own thing and not respecting God as King. He wants us to teach our children to obey Him rather than doing works.

It is wise to teach our kids to obey the laws of God and the laws of man (parents, local, state and federal).

I remember my four year old son was coughing and sneezing. I told him I thought he was getting sick and he just sat there quietly. My two year old daughter preceded to get in my son's face with her finger pointed and said, "Babel, you are going to the doctor!" At first, I wonder where she got that behavior but I soon recognized it. It was me!! I would also see generosity, helpfulness, kindness, but I also saw sarcasm, impatience and anger. I wanted to purposefully teach them the generosity, helpfulness and kindness but as they were watching me perform the nice things, they were watching me perform the sarcasm, impatience and the anger. I didn't want them to learn those unwanted things that I myself did not like but they did not stop watching me when I was acting crazy. In the sponge of their minds, they were soaking it all in and imitating me. They were also taking in my husband's behaviors. He can be very quiet and doesn't mind being alone. He can get angry and doesn't want to talk to you. My son, Basil, is the same way and it does not bother him to be alone and when he is mad at you, he is probably not going to talk to you much. None of my kids have had a lot of friends because I believe; neither my husband nor I have had a lot of friends. We are very select and they have become the same way. It is amazing the things we teach them, when we are not intentionally teaching them.

God is good all the time and all the time, God is good. He is the ultimate example of what a good parent should be and it is through Him we can do what is right by our kids. When they are learning obedience from a parent they can see, then they may do better at obeying one they cannot see with their eyes. They can know he is real is their hearts.

RESPECT AND HONOR

Do not rebuke an older man harshly, but exhort him as if he were your father. Treat younger men as brothers, 2older women as mothers, and younger women as sisters, with absolute purity.

1 Timothy 5:1-2

To exhort means to honor or to hold in high regard. So many of our youth today lack respect for those who are older. Although the Bible says we are to treat older men as fathers, the problem is, many kids don't have fathers in their lives that they've learned to respect. Also, there are those who have part-time dads, once-a-month dads, once-a-year dads, or, sadly, dads that show up only after they have become sick or old and want someone to take care of them. Some only show up when their children do something spectacular and they want recognition for being the fathers of such children.

Our society has made such a joke out of the position of dad. Many TV shows degrade the role of fathers. On these programs, the children disobey, disrespect, and demean their dads. The mothers do nothing to correct the situation and most times join in on the humiliation. Also, the men say things that make them look like clowns, while the mothers cheer the kids on in their bad behavior.

The sad thing is that wholesome shows from the past like *The Cosby Show, Leave it to Beaver, The Brady Bunch,* and *Father Knows Best* would probably not make it past one season today. Television people are all about money, and they give the people what they want. Shows that aren't watched are cancelled. There is so much lack of respect in so many programs, and it seems the more disrespect there is, the more successful the show.

In our culture today, many older women do not dress and act like women of character and modesty. Older women should teach the younger women how to act, how to dress, how to talk, and how to carry themselves as godly women of God. The Bible doesn't say that we treat people with respect only if they act respectfully. We are to treat people as they should be treated, not according to the way they act.

When Jesus met the woman, He treated her with respect.

The teachers of the law and the Pharisees brought in a woman caught in adultery. They made her stand before the group and said to Jesus, "Teacher, this woman was caught in the act of adultery. In the Law Moses commanded us to stone such women. Now what do you say?" They were using this question as a trap, in order to have a basis for accusing him. But Jesus bent down and started to write on the ground with his finger. When they kept on questioning him, he straightened up and said to them, "If any one of you is without sin, let him be the first to throw a stone at her." Again he stooped down and wrote on the ground. At this, those who heard began to go away one at a time, the older ones first, until only Jesus was left, with the woman still standing there. Jesus straightened up and asked her, "Woman, where are they? Has no one condemned you?" "No one, sir," she said. "Then neither do I condemn you," Jesus declared. "Go now and leave your life of sin."

John 8:3-11

(If she was caught in the act, where is the man that was there with her? Shouldn't the man have been brought before the people also?)

If younger women were treated as sisters, we wouldn't have the trafficking of young girls that we do. Also, the abuse of children by family members, neighbors, teachers, coaches, preachers, and others would not exist if we cared deeply for others and loved them. Society would love and respect all if we treated others the way we want to be treated according to the Word.

Rise in the presence of the aged, show respect for the elderly and revere your God. I am the Lord.

Leviticus 19: 32

Showing respect for the elderly and those who are our parents is paired with revering God. He then says, "I am the Lord" to let us know that it is He who is speaking. It is even stated to stand up in the presence of those who are older than we are. It's as though as we honor others, we honor the Lord. If we can't honor those whom we can see, how can we honor the Lord whom we cannot see?

"Honor your father and your mother, so that you may live long in the land the LORD your God is giving you.

Exodus 20:12

There is a promise that goes along with honoring parents. God will lengthen the days of the children who obey their parents who teach them according to Scripture. There is coverage in obedience. When this is not taught in the home, it is not good for the children. Children do not honor parents when they call them names, make wisecracks to them, use profanity with them, argue with them, or talk about them behind their backs. The truth is, although the parents may not hear, God does. It is also not good or respectful for parents to direct this type of behavior towards their children.

God will reward or punish children for their behavior towards their parents. If they have been taught this, it rest in their hands to prolong their lives. We must, therefore, guard against wanting a friendship with our kids so much that we let them speak to us in any way they want.

I once had this very situation going on in my house. My daughter said she loved her dad—and I knew that she did—but she was talking to him in just any way she wanted. If she had been honoring him, she would have treated him the way that she treated her teachers, neighbors, the president, or anyone else in authority. I got on her for this behavior and approached my husband about letting her do this. He wanted me to stay out of it, because, he said, if it didn't bother him, then it shouldn't bother me. But I knew it bothered God and that He does not excuse such behavior. I would not let the matter rest, and my daughter made changes in this area. Whether the parent allows a certain behavior or not, if it is against the Word of God, it is wrong.

Therefore, prepare your minds for action; be self-controlled; set your hope fully on the grace to be given you when Jesus Christ is revealed. 14As obedient children do not conform to the evil desires you had when you lived in ignorance. 15But just as he who called you is holy, so be holy in all you do; 17Show proper respect to everyone: Love the brotherhood of believers, fear God, honor the king.

1 Peter 2:13-15,17

If we teach honor and respect in the home, then it will spread outside the home. We are to honor all the authorities in our lives. The *only* time we do not obey authority is when it goes against the Word. Even if we don't like the person in authority, we must respect the position of one in authority. The Hebrew boys in the book of Daniel showed respect to the king, but they didn't obey him when he wanted them to bow to the idol of himself. They decided to suffer the consequences instead of obeying the king. Sometimes it will come to that point. But even with our parents, we can respect them without dishonoring our heavenly Father.

Honor the LORD with your wealth, with the firstfruits of all your crops; then your barns will be filled to overflowing, and your vats will brim over with new wine.

Proverbs 3:9-10

We must also honor God with all the material things that we own. We have them only because He has blessed us with all good gifts. Honor is not just about the people in our lives, but it is also about all things in our lives, including our money. We respect God as the giver of all that is good, and that includes our money, houses, and other material possessions.

I was raised to say "yes, ma'am" and "yes, sir" or "no, ma'am" and "no, sir." I was taught to respect and honor authority, but that did not include obeying someone who told me to do something contrary to the Word of God, my parents, or my own good judgment. My kids, too, have been taught to say "sir" and "ma'am," but they have also been instructed not to obey adults absolutely because not every adult will tell them the right thing to do. I want my children to listen to their own instincts, judgment, and discernment. That includes relationships with relatives. The foundation begins with the Word of God and builds from there.

If an adult tells my children to do something contrary to the Word of God or against the things that my husband and I have taught them, or if a certain behavior makes them feel uncomfortable, or if an adult wants to touch them in any way, they have been instructed to go against that authority. That person will no longer qualify to come near my children. My children will still be expected to show honor to them by saying "sir" and "ma'am," but that person has lost the right to expect obedience from them. If my children have a problem with the law, a government leader, a teacher, or a boss, they are expected to obey the rules as long as they are not contradictory to what they have been taught.

Just as we want respect from our children, our children want respect from us. My middle son once decided he needed to talk to my husband and me. He had taken a psychology class at school, and basically, he had been told to stand up to people who didn't respect him. He thought this applied to me, his mother, and the sad part was, he didn't feel comfortable speaking to me alone but needed my husband to be there with us. My son started out by saying he had no doubt that I loved him dearly. He acknowledged I took good care of him and wanted only the best for him.

However, he said, it did not seem that I respected him. Even though he was in the upper grades in high school, I was still making many decisions for him and not listening to his responses. I still thought of him as a kid, he said. He was right. He was not a little kid anymore, and he needed not only to make his own decisions but also to have those decisions respected.

This conversation hurt me like a knife, but I simply had to get alone for a couple of hours and talk to the Lord and let Him speak to me. He showed me that Basil was right, and He showed me the strength it took for my son to speak up and confront me. After the hurt cleared, I had so much respect for him. In the past, I had thought that he would always let other people push him around, but this action assured me he was able to stand up for himself. I wrote him a long letter (letter, because I wanted him to continually return to read my apology) and apologized, telling him the spectacular man I thought he had become. I apologized for disrespecting him; even though that had not been my intention, that was how he perceived it, and therefore that was his reality of the situation.

In our talk, Basil showed me how I often doubted the things he said, causing him to lose heart in saying anything. If a situation seemed to be a certain way, then I accused him of that action. Again, this was not my intention, but that was his reality, and therefore it was real to him. In the letter, I told him I was so proud of his boldness, and things became better between us because I asked the Lord to show me myself and He did.

I must say, even after the hurt, that meeting was freeing for both my son and me. I can see now how he could have interpreted my actions as disrespect. Respect was not the order of the day in the home I grew up in, nor was it in my grandparents' home. This is no excuse, only an explanation. I am responsible for my actions and what I pass on to my kids.

DISCIPLINE—TOUGH LOVE

Laws were put in place to show us where we are wrong so that we can give thought to our behavior. The Ten Commandments were recorded to show us what not to do. They are not suggestions, but commandments to live by. God loves us, and He wants us to live in harmony with His design. We can't just live without rules or guidelines. We have to know what is wrong so that we will know what is right.

We must show our children that there are consequences for their actions. We should teach our children to obey us and other adult authorities in their lives, whom they can see, as a precursor for obeying God, whom they cannot see. When we do that, we are teaching them to have faith.

On the other hand, we adults can be so headstrong about not obeying certain laws if we don't think they are necessary or if we don't agree with them. But how can we teach our children to obey the law if we ourselves are lawbreakers? We can't tell our children, "Do as I say, not as I do." Actions always speak louder than words.

Wisdom is found on the lips of the discerning but a rod is for the back of him who lacks judgment.

Proverbs 10:13

To teach wisdom to our children, we must seek God from whom all wisdom comes. We are so finite in what we know, but He is infinite. Our children will not learn merely from our words; sometimes they will require stern discipline. Sometimes we may have to let them fall before we can help them up, or else they may not learn the important lessons they need to learn. Those hard times may be what's needed to turn their lives around.

Then the mother of Zebedee's sons came to Jesus with her sons and kneeling down, asked a favor of him. "What is it you want?" he asked. She said," Grant that one of these two sons of mine may sit at your right and the other at your left in your kingdom." "You don't know what you are asking," Jesus to them. "Can you drink the cup I am going to drink?" "We can," they answered. Jesus said to them," You will indeed drink from the cup, but to sit at my right or left is not for me to grant. These places belong to those for whom they have been prepared by my Father."

Matthew 20: 20-23

We have to be careful in what and how we pray for our kids. We should always pray that God's will is done in their lives. The mother in the passage above wanted her kids to have seats of prestige, but she did not know what was entailed in that request. I'm sure she would not have wanted them to go through the suffering that Christ was going to endure if she had known what lay ahead.

Similarly, sometimes we see others in various positions and want badly for our children to attain the same success. However, we see only the finished work. We don't see the hard work, discipline, loss of rest and sleep, loss of socializing, and the many other things that were put on the back burner or taken totally off the stove to achieve the desired result. Furthermore, even if our children achieve the desired result, we forget that they will have to work to keep it. We will have to make sure they study hard, take care of their bodies, and watch what goes into their minds, and all of this may go against what their friends are doing.

My son, do not despise the LORD's discipline and do not resent his rebuke, because the LORD disciplines those he loves, as a father the son he delights in.

Proverbs 3:11

It is not easy being the parent of a child. I believe most parents mean well in their attempts to raise their children. But parenting is a road of uncertainty regarding choices and selections that we can only pray are right for a specific child's needs, dreams, and desires. Being the child is also difficult because at a certain point, most children think they know best. This may happen at the age of two, twelve, sixteen, or eighteen, but regardless of its timing, there's just something about independence that appeals to most of us.

Better is open rebuke than hidden love.

Proverbs 27:5

My son, do not despise the LORD's discipline and do not resent his rebuke, because the LORD disciplines those he loves, as a father the son he delights in.

Proverbs 3:11-12

So many parents are afraid to discipline their children. They want to be their children's friends or not hurt their children's feelings. Additionally, many teachers are paralyzed by fear and thus fail to discipline a child that clearly needs correcting. They are afraid they will be sued or reap some other negative consequence. Some may clearly love the children in their classes and want to set them on the right path, but they are told they can't.

Eli and his sons were punished by God for Eli's refusal to discipline his sons. They did wicked things in the temple, and although Eli knew of their misbehavior, he rebuked them but he did not remove the boys from their position in the church. (This story can be found in its entirety in 1 Samuel chapters 2–4).

Let a righteous man strike me—it is a kindness; let him rebuke me—it is oil on my head. My head will not refuse it.

Psalms 141:5

Consequences and punishment are good for adults as well as for youth. The police, teachers, neighbors, coaches, other parents, and many other people can counsel and correct us, and it will be a blessing. If we take heed, we can be guided onto a better road that will lead to less strife in our lives. If discipline is done in a respectful manner, our children will learn that we mean them well in their punishment.

When I was young, I had neighbors who would let my mother know if they saw my siblings or me doing something we shouldn't be doing. Once I pushed my brother off an eight-to-ten-foot porch. He was only in the first or second grade. I thought I had gotten away with it, but my neighbor ran over and told my mother. I hadn't even noticed her presence, and I couldn't believe she told on me this way. However, from that point on, I would check to see if I was being watched when I played outside. Even at church, there were members watching other members' kids.

Some parents today will jump down your throat if you tell them something negative about their children. They want you to stay out of their business and leave their children alone. That is the problem: they are leaving their children alone and want everyone else to leave them alone too. It used to be people would be thanked for letting parents know if they saw their children doing something wrong, and hopefully, the parents would then talk to their children to get their side of the story. Yeah, yeah, I know, some are saying the talking part didn't happen in their house, but wouldn't it have been nice? I think it is good for children to know that someone is watching them. Some don't realize that God is watching at all times and sees all their deeds. They need to know that even if parents or others do not see and punish them, God sees and will punish with His loving hand. Tough love is good.

Those whom I love I rebuke and discipline. So be earnest, and repent.

Revelations 3:19

God loves us too much to let us stay in our sinful ways. He created us for His purposes, and He knows what is best for each individual. I love my children, and I have always considered which of their behaviors might negatively affect their future. Many people, however, think it is cute for their children to curse, hit their parents, or do other vulgar and disrespectful things. Many parents have taught their kids not to say "yes, ma'am" and "no, sir." But what's wrong with giving honor where honor is due? What's wrong with giving honor to our elders whether in age or position? Some may say that certain people do not deserve it, but God wants us to call those things that are not as though they are.

We have to do this with our children and stop hitting the replay button on their mistakes. We must let them know of the future we see for them. If we don't see a specific future, we can at least convince them that they can make their own future prosperous and successful. Prosperity and success are different for everyone. It may or may not include a lot of money. But it should definitely include treating other people with kindness and respect.

It is good for a man to bear the yoke while he is young.

Lamentations 3:27

Kids need to work and earn money. Even younger children need to do chores around the house. It teaches them responsibility and gives them a sense of accomplishment. They learn to take pride in a job well done. It also teaches them submission to authority. People appreciate things more when they have to work for them. It is not good for children to get everything they want. Even if they can afford everything after they are adults, they still shouldn't have everything they want.

I grew up in a home where discipline was definitely and absolutely administered. Looking back, I feel it did go to the extreme most of the time. When I had children of my own, I initially administered the same type of extreme discipline. I thought that was the way kids should be corrected because that was what I remembered from my childhood. When my husband had seen enough of my harsh treatment, he spoke up to defend the kids. I believe this shows one reason why children need both a father and a mother.

This unhealthy pattern of discipline was modeled even in the adult relationships in my family. I remember my grandfather hitting my mother, and in the early 1990s, she in turn struck me in the face, even though I was a married adult. I was so angry with her and had to make adjustments in our relationship for a while, setting up boundaries to protect myself. I didn't want to retaliate in like manner and dishonor her.

I do, however, believe in punishment directed to the seat of the pants of a child who needs correction, but there is a line that should not be crossed. I am ashamed to say I have gotten up close in my oldest son's face, who was eighteen years old at the time, self-righteously spilling out threats. But the older I got, the more I could see the benefits of calming down and thinking and listening before administering punishment. I saw this example in my husband, and I could see that the response he received from the kids was very different from mine. On the other hand, my husband would sometimes get mad and not want to speak to the children at all; then I would have to talk with him about his reaction. Despite all my mistakes, the good thing is, the more I stayed in the Word, the more I was convicted of my behavior and the damage I was doing to my children.

Corporal punishment was such a common occurrence to me that I didn't immediately recognize potential abuse when a child in a church class I was teaching showed up with bruises. In my mind, I excused it as nothing out of the ordinary. I did come to my senses before the class was over and report it to a deacon and to the pastor. Honestly, I don't know what happened in this particular case, but corporal punishment that goes too far is a sad legacy of many families and cultures.

Appropriate forms of corporal punishment may need to be practiced in raising young children, but not in disciplining older teens and adults. Of course, there are time when the answer no should stay no. Children can't and should not get everything they want, even if it is within our power as parents to give it. My husband and I did not have much when we were growing up because we were poor, but although we have the capability to get our children many of the things they want, we set limits. It is good for some wants to stay wants. Children need to learn the benefit of saving for what they want and practicing patience as they wait for it.

PROTECT AND GUARD

It is our job to protect our children. They have a God-given right to be protected from physical, mental, social, or spiritual harm. We have to pray and be watchful at all times because the enemy is always looking for opportunities to attack us and our children. If we are not careful about protecting ourselves from harm, then we won't be equipped to watch over the treasures that God has given us in the form of our children.

But understand this: If the owner of the house had known at what time of night the thief was coming, he would have kept watch and would not have let his house be broken into. So you also must be ready because the Son of Man will come at an hour when you do not expect him.

Matthew 24: 43 & 44

We don't know when a thief is making plans to attack, but we can be sure that the enemy of our souls will always have a plan to attack us and our families. He walks around as a roaring lion, seeking whom he may devour. Satan's intent is not just to do harm or kill, but it is to totally consume or annihilate us.

However, we can be victorious in this battle against him, for the weapons of our warfare are not carnal, worldly, or visible, but they are mighty in God for pulling down strongholds. We have to guard and keep our hearts with all diligence, for out of the heart spring the issues of life (Prov. 4:23). We don't have to always be on our knees to pray, or have our hands pressed together and our eyes closed. We can pray to God at all times, even in the midst of working, cooking, cleaning, washing the car, taking a shower, and so forth.

We should pray for our children before they are born, pray about their future friends when they are only two months old, and even pray about their future dates and eventual spouses when they are just three years old or younger. While we are praying for them, we should be teaching them what the Word of God says about each subject.

We should also live what we are teaching our children. They will more quickly imitate what they see than what they hear. We won't be perfect examples for them, but we can explain things to them at the appropriate time. It is also very important to apologize if we have harmed them in some way or failed to protect them when we should have. Sometimes, just admitting to our failures will protect them from future incidents in their lives. We can let them know that we love them, even though we may not love everything they do. We can confirm in them that we will love them forever and always, just as Jesus loves us even though He doesn't like all the choices we make.

Who shall separate us from the love of Christ? Shall trouble or hardship or persecution or famine or nakedness or danger or sword? No, in all these things we are more than conquerors through Him who loved us.

Romans 8:35 & 37

We have the assurance that Christ's love for us is constant. Sometimes, when our children aren't sure of our love for them, they will join other groups to feel loved and connected. Many of these groups aren't safe or good for them. We don't need to win every battle with our children but lose the war in the process. Is it really worth it to win every argument, just so we can say we won, but leave our children feeling beaten down?

No, that is not the way. Rather, we should treasure these dear ones who have been given to us through birth or adoption. Yes, they may sometimes do things wrong, but then so do we. God forgives us and accepts us still, and we must extend to our children the same love and acceptance that He extends to us. Proverbs 10:12 says that love covers all sins. That does not mean that everything done is fine and acceptable. But it does mean that forgiveness and acceptance can be found when genuine love exists between people.

Set a guard over my mouth, O Lord; keep watch over the door of my lips. Let not my heart be drawn to what is evil, to take part in wicked deeds with men who are evildoers; let me not eat of their delicacies.

Psalms. 141: 3&4

We have to consciously decide not to say everything that comes to our minds to our children. We really do have to ask God to put a guard on our lips, because once words are spoken, they cannot be taken back. They leave an imprint on the minds of the hearers. Though this truth can be used for the bad, it can also be used for the good. When we encourage our children and speak good words over them, we cover them with love and put a guard over their lives and their minds. This will help them when others come against them in negative ways. With our words, we can be either the wind beneath their wings or the lack thereof that causes them to never take off or to come crashing to the ground.

I began my early education in the mid sixties. I heard many bad things spoken against my race, my family, and myself. Those bad words came from the schools and teachers, from people in stores, people in church, and people in my own extended family. I heard society declare that those of my race were dumb and would never amount to anything. The educational system affirmed it by letting me see a school with good books, nice desks, and clean walls and restrooms and then transferring me to a school that was the total opposite. Some not-so-nice teachers told us black kids we had nothing to be proud of and black power was nothing. My church whispered that I was nothing because I was one of eight children born to a single mother. Also, I had extended family members who called us bastards because we had no father in our home. I had to fight subconsciously to feel even a little bit good about myself.

I did, however, have relatives who made all the difference in my world: my mother, my grandmother, and my grandfather. Linitia and Jeffery, my older siblings, were also protective and generous to me and my younger siblings.

My mother was a firm woman at times, but she could put me on cloud nine other times. She was very protective of her children, and not many people were allowed to hang around us. She told us to play with one another, and she would go outside and play kick ball, dodge ball, and many other games that people don't remember anymore. She took us on picnics, to the movies, to the circus, and to other places.

My grandparents also spent time with us. Grandmother helped to take care of us when we were sick, but she also did fun things with us. When it was raining, Granddaddy was always outside our house in the morning and at the school in the afternoon to transport us back and forth. Nobody ever asked him to do it—he was just always there.

I also recall an abusive relationship my mother was once in, and though the man didn't hurt us kids, he did hurt our mother. That hurt me as much as if I had been the one abused. I also heard about abused kids, how some were killed by the very people left in charge to protect them. As a result of this background, I have always been protective of my own children. If I can help them in any way, then I will, as long as it does not hinder their growth and maturity. By the time children are adults, however, prayer is often the only help that can be rendered.

In my first marriage, my husband was very abusive. He would hit and kick me and call me the most horrible names. Nevertheless, I tried to make our home a happy one for my son's sake. When my son was only four months old, I suffered my worst abuse incident at the hands of my husband. I had gone to a Bible study, and when I came home, I went into the bedroom to put the baby to sleep. I didn't realize that my husband had followed me until I was pushed to the ground and was lying on my back.

My husband then jumped on me and began to hit me in my face. When I saw his fist coming towards my face, I began to call on Jesus. I did feel the first hit, but I did not feel the other eight to ten punches to my face. In fact, my face should have been swollen, battered, and bloody, but its appearance never changed. I think this confused him; he wanted to draw blood, but it didn't happen. He looked so confused, then got up and left the room.

I put the baby to sleep and went to a corner store to call the friends that I had been in Bible study with earlier. I told them what had happened and asked them to call the police to come and take me away. The police arrived at my home, and I left my husband that night and never returned. During the time I was away, I decided I didn't want my baby boy to grow up around this person, and I didn't want him to see his dad hitting his mom. I knew how damaging this was to children.

It is not good for kids to see a parent, male or female, being abused physically, mentally, verbally, emotionally, socially, or in any other way. I wanted the tolerance of this type of abusive behavior to stop with me. I didn't want my son to experience and possibly imitate the behavior he saw in his biological dad. I thus divorced my husband, and the judge gave me full custody and awarded me child support that I never collected. I decided I would rather pull myself up without my ex-husband's help. Even though I was weak and didn't press charges, the state of Georgia did, and he went to jail and served time.

I put a great deal of my life on hold to ensure the safety of my children. Looking back, I probably was somewhat overprotective. However, I would rather have to apologize to my kids for being around them too much than to have to apologize for something happening because I wasn't there.

Some of my family members were not left alone with my kids. Just because someone is family does not mean he or she is safe company for your kids. In fact, most kids are hurt by relatives or close neighbors because these are the ones given free access to them. It is even sadder when the children report the abuse to another family member who does nothing and tells them to keep the matter quiet and in the family. Sometimes these children are even blamed for the mistreatment they suffered. Such children grow up with many problems, and they in turn will affect the generations to come.

I must admit there were a few teachers along the way who did have a positive effect on me. A woman in the youth department at my church paid me a lot of positive attention. Barbara was always very complimentary to me, always telling me I was beautiful and would do good things with my life. I also remember a neighbor across the street from us who always spoke positive words to me.

It does take a village to raise a child, and it also takes more than a family to watch over and protect a child.

THE GIFT OF CHILDREN

Children are a gift from God, given to us for only a season. They belong to God, and we are to be good stewards of them, taking that responsibility seriously. Some children result from ugly situations, like pearls formed within oysters. These children may be the products of all sorts of abuse done to their mothers, and some of the mothers may not be able to properly handle the correlation between the child and the event. For many reasons, I didn't care to be around my ex-husband, but none of this related to my son. I loved my son, but in my head, I had to separate him from his father. They are two different individuals, and therefore I could love my son dearly despite who his father was.

When Jesus saw this, he was indignant. He said to them," Let the little children come to me, and do not hinder them, for the kingdom of God belongs to such as these.

Mark 10:14

Children were, and are, very special to the Lord. He likes everything about them, especially their innocence, inquisitiveness, and curiosity, as well as their easy ability to forgive, to show love, and to let go of anger. Jesus likes children so much that He wants all of us to be childlike, but not childish. He wants us to possess many of the attributes of children, but to be mature in the knowledge and actions of the Word.

But wisdom is proved right by all her children.

Luke 7: 35

Wisdom reproduces from itself, or her likeness is shown in her children. That means there will be signs of her attributes in her children. When someone says to a kid, "You act just like your daddy [or your mama]," is it an insult or a compliment? Can people see why a daughter is so mouthy, when they meet her mother? Can they see why a son fights and is abusive, when they meet his father? Can they see why some children are cheaters, liars, thieves, or wild, when they meet their parents?

It also works the other way. When others see the kindness and generosity of a child, they know why when they see the parent. However, an oddity sometimes exists when parent and child are totally different in behavior. Sometimes a generous parent has a very selfish and self-centered child, or a caring child has mean parents.

Her children arise and call her blessed; her husband also, and he praises her.

Proverbs 31:28

This verse comes from Proverbs 31, which is about women. The woman in this chapter faithfully took care of her home and family with precise care. What will our children say about us? Will they thank us as they grow up? Will they say, "Thank you for being there for me and keeping me on track"? Will they say, "My parents were firm, but I knew they loved me. They did punish me, and I didn't get everything I wanted, but I knew they cared"? Believe it or not, kids need structure and discipline. I believe they even want it, on a certain level, because it tells them that someone cares about them and what they do.

Children's children are a crown to the aged, and parents are the pride of their children.

Proverbs 17:6

Grandparents so enjoy their grandchildren. They can have so much fun with them but then send them home. But if we have not given our children the tools they need to be successful in life, they will not have anything to pass down to their children. Grandchildren aren't a crown if they haven't been raised properly. Instead, they are a thorny crown that makes our hair stand up on our necks at the very thought of them. No one wants to show off something he or she is embarrassed about. Also, as is mentioned in this Scripture, children want to be proud of their parents.

Sons are a heritage from the Lord, children a reward from him. Like arrows in the hands of a warrior are sons born in one's youth. Blessed is the man whose quiver is full of them.

Psalms 127:3-5

Children are a blessing, and they reward our lives in many ways. They all bring their own set of blessings, and when there are many children in a family, there are many blessings as well. Unfortunately, some people don't see children as blessings.

I definitely think kids are gifts, because during my first marriage, I was told there was a 98 to 99 percent chance I would never have kids. My first husband had given me PID (pelvic inflammatory disease), and by the time I went to the doctor and discovered why I was so sick, my female organs had been badly scarred. But despite the odds, God blessed me and I conceived.

Initially, the pregnancy caught me off guard; I was happy, but overwhelmed. The thought of a baby and the accompanying responsibility weighed heavily on my mind because at the time I barely had a place to lay my own head. The situation in my marriage was horrible, and I was down on life and living. But when my first son, Brandon, was born, he gave me a reason to live. I immediately thought of the importance of doing right by this child, keeping him safe, keeping him well, giving him love though I was running on empty myself.

During the pregnancy, times were hard, and I was practically homeless. I was quite scared for this child I was carrying. But it was no longer just me that I had to consider, so I shifted into a different gear. A precious gift was on its way, and I had to prepare. I experienced both excitement and anxiety all at the same time. I wanted to do this as right as I could. I made many mistakes in the process, but I was figuring things out as I went along.

Another reason I believe children are gifts from God stems from an abortion I had when I was in my twenties. This occurred after my first husband, but before my present one. I was pregnant and I could think only of not being able to support two children. I should not have been doing what it took to get pregnant in the first place! I was depressed and alone and I didn't appreciate the gift that was growing within me. I paid for that life to be snuffed out before it ever had a chance. Yes, I was pro-choice, and my choice cost that precious one its life. I now believe that once we conceive a child, the right choice is to give that little one a chance. I wish all the pro-life people would put down their signs and open places to help mothers-to-be make the right choice. And I wish they would actually be there for them in life.

I was meant to be a steward over this gift, but I violated that responsibility in the worst possible way. Consumed with self-centered thoughts, I couldn't handle what was happening. All I could think was that I couldn't handle this pregnancy, which I couldn't afford to feed, clothe, and provide day care for yet another child. It was just too much, and I was overwhelmed. I wish there had been someone to help me make sense of my life at the time, but there was not. I wish I had thought about the fact that if my own mother had not been a pro-life believer, I would not have been alive.

For years after the abortion, I could hear the child calling to me. I could hear a baby crying, and I could not escape the guilt. It took me nearly fifteen years to finally feel the forgiveness of the Lord. It was not that He didn't offer it from day one—I just couldn't accept it. The problem was in me. I let the enemy consume me and taunt me for years with unbearable guilt and shame. I don't want to sound arrogant now in saying that I'm free of this, but God has forgiven me and given me the voice to testify to other women considering this action or who have already taken it.

At the time I became pregnant, I was hungry for attention. The guy was supposed to be a Christian, a deacon, and he was soon to be ordained. He would not even take me to church with him. He told a lot of lies that I fell for and believed but I think it was because I was so alone.

But when attention is needed, even the bitter seems sweet. I was at a point where I felt I was literally dying for attention and touch. This guy was a corrections officer and not that nice to me. Nevertheless, I would take a bus and then the train just to see him. I went through all of that because I thought he would be a good example for my son. He was not, but I had to hit rock bottom to see this.

When I told him I was pregnant, he didn't seem interested. I then decided I was on my own, because I was not going home to my mother. The decision to have the abortion was one of the most difficult decisions that I have ever made in my entire life. The few people that I confided in did not try to talk me out of it. When the father found out that I had gotten an abortion, he said he couldn't believe I had done that. I told him I didn't want to see him again. Most times I try to learn from my mistakes and not repeat the cycle. I remembered the way I felt on the day I got the abortion, and I knew I would never do that again.

Concerning abortion, I have a pet peeve with both major political parties. The party against abortion loudly protests against a woman getting rid of her child—and I agree that is wrong—but they do nothing to help the woman who decides to have the baby. They don't seem to care whether the child has enough food to eat, clothes to wear, or protection from harm. They resent programs that provide for such children to start school early, receive an education that includes tutoring and after-school care, and be awarded scholarships and grants for college. They also oppose tax relief for middle- and low-income families, disability benefits, social security benefits, workers' compensation, Medicaid, or any other kind of aid for the poor or disadvantaged. They would rather stay on their high horse and judge those who need this kind of help.

The other political party is just the opposite. They not only approve of a woman's choice to have her child killed but also want others to pay for it. But I believe life begins at conception, so why should I have to pay for someone's decision to kill her child? This party also wants taxpayers to pay for condoms and birth control pills for adolescents. Should I be forced to pay for someone else's night of wild fun or the consequences resulting from it?

Why can't parents be more diligent in teaching their children abstinence? Why don't we teach it more in schools? Our kids would really like to hear from their parents more about sex and other sex related topics. We have to stop being nervous and scared to discuss things for fear of encouraging them or just plain ole fear.

It seems that people today are taught to be victims instead of victors in life, discouraged from having dreams and going after them. Things are not always easy, but we can encourage others not to give up. We can encourage them to get a hand up or even a handout when needed. We can help them see the consequences of their actions.

We can all accomplish many things in life because God has a plan for each one of us. I believe that with God all things are possible for me. I can do all things through Christ who gives me strength.

PROVOKE NOT TO ANGER

When we show anger, we are reacting to something or someone. The anger was already there; it was just pulled out of us

Fathers, do not exasperate your children; instead, bring them up in the training and instruction of the Lord.

Ephesians 6:4

Father, do not embitter you children, or they will become discouraged.

Colossians 3:21

To exasperate is to make angry or to irritate on purpose. *To embitter* is to make bitter or to arouse bitter feelings. *To discourage* is to deprive someone of confidence, hope, or spirit; it means to hamper or hinder. As parents, why would we intentionally do any of these things to our children? I don't believe that it is always done intentionally. I love my children, but I know for a fact that sometimes I have made them angry and bitter to the point that they became discouraged.

A gentle answer turns away wrath, but a harsh word stirs up anger.

Proverbs 15:1

I'm a loud person with a big mouth, and in dealing with my children, I seldom thought before I spoke words that I later regretted. I never used profanity, and I never called them names. Though I never said I didn't love them, my words were hurtful nonetheless. Basically, I am a screamer with a high-pitched voice. Many times the pitch of my voice made it seem as though I was lambasting them, even when that was not my intention.

The spoken word is one thing that cannot be taken back. My fussing, accusing, and being loud could have ruined my children's lives, had it not been for their dad and the conviction of the Holy Spirit. In my defense, I never meant to incite my children to anger, but I was driven by an overzealous spirit that wanted to raise smart, obedient, Christian children. Many times I also operated from fear over their safety. To this day, I'm still apologizing to my children as certain events come to mind. I am still praying and trying to repair our relationship.

And because the Lord had closed her womb, her rival kept provoking her in order to irritate her. her rival provoked her till she wept and would not eat

1 Samuel 1:6&7b

    This Scripture is talking about Hannah, Samuel's mother. "Her rival provoked her till she wept and would not eat," and in verse 8, the Bible says she was downhearted. Hannah was in this state, not because of her own doing, but because of what the Lord had allowed. The woman Peninnah was stealing Hannah's joy and having fun at her expense because of something beyond Hannah's ability to change. In a similar fashion, do we pick at and provoke our children because of something they can't even change? Do we try to force them to perform in ways totally against their natural bent? What if we keep trying to bend them and they break in the process? What then?

    Sadly, there are some parents who intentionally choose to provoke and incite anger in their children for combative reasons. I am so sorry for the children who have to go through this, and prayerfully, they will be able to move on as adults. But it is not always a parent that provokes a child. Sometimes it is a teacher, neighbor, older sibling, or an intimidating, bullying person.

    Galatians 6:1 instructs us, "Brothers, if someone is caught in a sin, you who are spiritual should restore him gently." Why can't we start by applying this to our children? The Bible does speak of using the rod, but that is when all else fails. As Proverbs 13:24 says, "He who spares the rod hates his son, but he who loves him is careful to discipline him." This does not mean disciplining excessively and beyond measure, and it certainly does not mean constantly throwing the bad behavior into the child's face. Sometimes we must pray and let the Holy Spirit convict our children of sins and wrongdoings. He will do a much better job than we will. I'm not saying that we shouldn't say anything to our children when they do wrong, but I am saying to add prayer and fasting to the mix.

Luke 11:17 says, "Any house divided against itself will be ruined, and a house divided against itself will fall." When we work against our children or our spouses, then we are tearing down ourselves. When we continually push the buttons that agitate certain family members, then we are at war against them to our own detriment.

So let's build each other up, and that includes our children. God speaks a lot about love, and that is what we need in our families.

Love is patient, love is kind. It does not envy, it does not boast, it is not proud. It is not rude, it is not self-seeking, it is not easily angered, it keeps not records of wrongs, Love does not delight in evil but rejoices with the truth. It always protects, always trusts, always hopes, always perseveres. Love never fails.

1 Corinth 13: 4-8a

Love never fails!

Since we adults exert power over our children, we should always proceed with caution in using force to make them do something. We are smarter than they are, and we should use our intelligence to help us make wise decisions concerning them. We can usually get what we want and still leave them with their pride intact. Unfortunately, this wasn't done for me when I was a child, and I didn't do it with my children. Bullying or force was the method I was accustomed to, but it did not work all the time, either for me or for my kids.

Looking back now, I wish I had taken the time to explain situations to my kids while still standing by my convictions. I wish I had left them with some pride and helped them understand my decisions. Again, yes, I would have stood by most of my decisions, but not so harshly. I wish I had operated in love more often because love never fails.

Children do have to learn that they can't have their way all the time, but when their parents purposely do things to make them angry, that certainly doesn't help them learn. There are, indeed, parents who do things just to make their kids angry or to get a negative response out of them. This is provoking! This behavior on a parent's part causes their children to sin, and God is not pleased with that.

There is a difference between our kids getting angry because they don't like a decision that we have made and our intentionally pushing buttons that we know make them angry.

THEIR GIFTS—NOT OUR DREAMS

We have so many dreams in our heads for our kids that we want them to fulfill. Sometimes it is something we have always envisioned them doing, while other times it is something we have always wanted to do ourselves. But 1 Corinthians 7:6 clearly says, "Each man has his own gift from God; one has this gift, another has that." We are all individuals, and God has a plan for each and every one of us. He has given each of us the grace that we need to accomplish the gift or gifts He has placed in us. The grace is for the accomplishment of our gifts, not for what someone else wants for us. If we are forced into molds that we were never intended for, we will lack the sense of purpose and fulfillment found in pursuing the innate gifts.

Romans 11:29 says, "For God's gifts and his call are irrevocable." You see, He does not change His mind concerning the things we were created to do. I've heard of doctors and lawyers quitting their professions for jobs that didn't pay as much but provided much more fulfillment. Also, some people have quit jobs that didn't pay much and went on to become doctors and lawyers, finding fulfillment in that.

Pass the Blessings!

It is not always about the money. It is fine for us to have money as long as money does not have us. It is not always money that will open the doors for us.

I believe that our gifts are not intended just for ourselves but also for the good of others. There are things that I can't do for myself and need others to do for me, and there are things I can do to assist others that they cannot do on their own. Doctors need store clerks, and store clerks need doctors. Engineers need garbage collectors, and garbage collectors need engineers. Police officers need teachers, and teachers need police officers. Farmers need truck drivers, and truck drivers need farmers.

We need each other!

We must know and believe there is a plan for each of our lives, and it is a good one. I do now have a bachelor's in ministry, but I only wanted it for the deeper knowledge I would gain from the Word of God. I feel this was more beneficial for God's plan for me than a traditional college degree. God can work through all of us in different ways and work for good. Sometimes, however, we can feel disappointed if we compare ourselves with others. We can't work out others' life plans—only our own.

For I know the plans I have for you" declares the Lord," plans to prosper you and not to harm you, plans to give you hope and a future. Then you will call me and come and pray to me, and I will listen to you. You will seek me and find me when you seek me with all your heart. I will be found by you," declares the Lord,"

Jeremiah 29:11 – 14

According to Jeremiah, there are definite plans for all of us, plans for good and not bad, plans to give us hope for the future. God knows the future, and there is hope. Hope does not mean there won't be hard times; it does mean that He will be with us. We must call on Him to help us, and we must pray this over our children.

The next two Scriptures say that we should talk to the Lord and also to many wise Christians.

Commit to the Lord whatever you do, and your plans will succeed.

Proverbs 16:3

Plans fail for lack of counsel, but with many advisors they succeed.

Proverbs 15:22

I had dreams for each and every one of my kids. I thought I knew what was best for them as they moved forward. For example, my daughter, who still lives at home, has the size and height of a good basketball player, and this was good exercise for her, I thought. So for many years I routinely signed her up for basketball. It didn't matter whether she enjoyed the sport—I wanted it to happen. She did try to like it, since she often heard me claim she would one day be in the WNBA. However, it was not a part of her deep down inside. Whether it was the sport itself or the exertion it required, she didn't love basketball like I wanted her to. At the same time, however, she was studying the flute, and she loved it. She is now excelling in the marching band and the symphonic band. I must admit, though, that this past basketball season took a toll on our relationship!

My second son was so smart that he taught himself to read when he was between two and three years of age. He scored in the ninety-seventh and ninety-eighth percentiles of the Georgia CRCT (Criterion-Referenced Competency Test) test. He was even passing his tests at school without doing the daily homework, until I found out about it. So my husband and I had to make sure he did not neglect the seemingly less important things like homework, projects, and essays.

Although he managed to do very well in school, my husband and I chose not to enroll him in a magnet school or accelerated courses because of his lack of motivation to do the necessary work. He did take piano lessons from first grade until eleventh grade, but it was a fight the whole way. He played the piano well and performed many times throughout those years, but it was just never something he really wanted to do. Looking back, do I wish we had pushed him anyway into accelerated classes? Well, there are times when I regret the decision not to push him more, but he has still done well and made us proud with the route that he has taken.

My oldest son loved the spotlight and always participated in talent shows, plays, public speaking, and guitar playing. But when he announced that he wanted to major in music in college, my husband and I told him that was not going to happen. Do I regret making that decision? Not really, because he didn't even show a strong interest in music until midway through the eleventh grade. Although he had taken music lessons since the fourth grade, we had to constantly force him to practice. Also, we could not see how a music degree would enable him to live independently. So he obtained a degree in psychology and sociology, but music remained an important part of his life throughout his college days and to today. We are proud of him and his accomplishments.

There was a period in my life when I wasted a lot of time coveting someone else's gift. I was part of a singing group from the time I was fifteen or sixteen until I was thirty-six years old. For years, I tried to sing second soprano. A friend of mine named Vanessa had a beautiful voice and could sing second soprano as well as other voice parts, and I wanted to sing like her. I wasted so much time coveting her gift, because the fact is, I don't sing well enough to call myself a singer. It is amazing that I let twenty years of my life go by pursuing something that was not my real gift. You see, although we may want something as a gift, if it is not really our gift, then we are just wasting our time. I do admit that the group was a good cause, and the Christians in the group helped me in many ways in my life. Looking back, perhaps I should have still been in the group, but just played a different role.

There are times we will want so much for our kids to succeed at what we think they ought to do. It could be something they don't want to do and have no interest in doing. Sometimes people ruin their relationships with their children because they are so pushy and dogmatic about their visions for their children's future. There will be times when our kids will not want to do something just because we want them to. We have to respect their wishes. Maybe if we back off, they will see that it is something they actually want to do.

Just because Great-granddaddy did it, and Granddaddy did it, and you are doing it, your child does not have to do it too. What if everyone else in the family went to college but your child does not want to go? Believe me, that would be a very hard thing for me to accept. However, if trying to force a child to do something ruins your relationship with that child, it is not worth it. It is also not worth it if the child is unhappy with a decision you force on him or her. We don't always know what is best for them. Also, we must make sure we don't withhold our affection from them if they don't do what we want them to do. Rules without relationship lead to rebellion!

BAD COMPANY

There is a saying that states, "Show me your friends, and I will tell you about you." We will usually act like the people we hang around with, sooner or later. We may start out not liking the things they do, but they will become more acceptable to us as time passes.

Proverbs speaks of the results of having either good friends or bad friends.

He who walks with the wise grows wise, but a companion of fools suffers harm.

Proverbs 13:20

He who keeps the law is a discerning son, but a companion of gluttons disgraces his father.

Proverbs 28: 7

A man of many companions may come to ruin, but there is a friend who sticks closer than a brother

Proverbs 18: 24

A bad friend can cause you to suffer harm, disgrace, and ruin. Who would do this intentionally to himself or herself? I don't believe anyone would, but it happens so often because of the associations we allow in our inner circles.

Do not make friends with a hot tempered man, do not associate with one easily angered or you may learn his ways and get yourself ensnared.

Proverbs 22:24

Again, you learn the ways of the people you hang around, like a student with a teacher. In a perfect world, we should not like hanging around bad people because of the things they do and say. We should love the things that God loves and hate the things that He hates.

He keeps company with evildoers; he associates with wicked men. For he says, it profits a man nothing when he tries to please God.

Job 34:8 & 9

Sometimes, when hanging around the wrong people, we eventually wonder about the benefits of living a life that pleases God. It may seem like certain people have all the fun and get away without living for Christ, but if the Lord came in an instant, they would be lost. Their fun is temporary, but our fun is eternal. We may face hard times in living for Christ, but He makes all things work for our good.

Do not envy wicked men, nor desire their company; for their hearts plot violence and their lips talk about making trouble.

Proverbs 24: 1 & 2

For the company of the godless will be barren, and fire will consume the tents of those who love bribes. They conceive trouble and give birth to evil; their womb fashion deceit.

Job 15:34 & 35

We should not want what wicked men have, because we don't know how they came to have it. They may have better homes, cars, clothes, friends, and many other things. Those things always look better if we don't know the whole story or see the whole picture. Such people may even seem like good people, but if they are without God, then they are still lost. They may give birth to seemingly good things, but not God things. What are their motives and intentions for the good that they get?

As iron sharpens iron, so one man sharpens another.

Proverbs 27:17

When we hang around good people who have hope and goals for the future, it encourages us to do better in our own lives. It's as though they shine a light on our own behavior. Negative people pull us down in thoughts, deeds, outlooks, abilities, friendships, wants and desires, sense of humor, the way we dress, and the list goes on and on.

Is not the whole land before you? Let's part company. If you go the left, I'll go to the right, if you go to the right, I'll go to the left.

Genesis 13:9

We even have to be careful about the family members we keep close company with. Sad to say, I could not allow my kids to hang around all my family members. I definitely didn't leave them alone with certain ones. I didn't want anyone making bad deposits into their spirits. I knew that certain things could be seen on some of their televisions, some profanity might be used, undesirable company might be allowed, or some wouldn't be as watchful and careful with my children as I would. It did not bother me if they were offended; my kids' safety was my priority.

Several years ago, I became friends with a woman at my job. She was very flirtatious with the men in the company and even with my own husband. Since I was hanging around her, the men at work thought I was like her, even though I was married. This woman was a nice person, and I enjoyed her friendship in many other ways. But after weighing everything, I decided to end the relationship because she was just not good for me or my family.

My daughter has had many friends that I immediately knew were not people I wanted her to hang around. When she was younger, I just did not let her do things with those I deemed inappropriate. As she grew older, I warned her about them and described behaviors that they manifested that were not good. She often protested that I thought badly about all her friends, but she wanted girlfriends that were exciting. I knew what I had taught my daughter and what she had learned in church. If any of these values were instilled in her, she would not be able to stay friends with these girls for long. So I watched, and to my amazement, these girls were soon no longer in my daughter's life. They talked ugly about other people and hurt others' feelings, and they did things that didn't feel right to my daughter. She soon started to make better choices about her friends and now associates with girls who have tastes similar to hers.

My oldest son went to college as a Christian, but in his third year there, he changed. The Christian people he associated with were not consistent in their walk. He started going places with others just for the sake of company, but their lives slowly became his. Additionally, many of his required classes for his psychology degree were contradictory to the Bible, and he worked closely with various psychology professors whose arguments against the Bible were not scientifically or spiritually correct. Loneliness and the influence of other people took a toll on him, and he soon succumbed to the pressure.

It is important to consider the people you hang around with because you will take on their ways.

RESPONSIBLE FOR ACTIONS
(Responsibility to Raise and Correct Our Children According to God's Word)

Even a child is known by his actions, by whether his conduct is pure and right.

Proverbs 20:11

It is important to consider the people we hang around because we will take on their ways. We will all be judged by our actions. There is an old saying that goes, "What you do speaks so loudly I can't hear a word you say." People will judge us by our actions even before they get to know us. We are responsible for our actions, and we cannot lay the blame for what we do on others. Our children tend to judge us by what we say, but we sometimes disappoint them with our actions.

—because she has rebelled against me,'" declares the LORD.
18"Your own conduct and actions have brought this upon you. This is your punishment.

How bitter it is! How it pierces to the heart!"

Jeremiah 4:17b-18

Our actions have consequences, and we will reap what we sow. Our actions are like seeds planted that will produce a harvest at some point. Good seed produces good fruit, and bad seed produces bad fruit.

I the LORD have spoken. The time has come for me to act. I will not hold back; I will not have pity, nor will I relent. You will be judged according to your conduct and your actions, declares the Sovereign LORD.'

Ezekiel 24:14

God has spoken, and it is up to us to obey. We are not just to know the Word, but we are also expected to obey it. If we choose to disobey, then, when it is time for punishment, we may get what we deserve. If we don't get what we deserve, it is only by the grace and mercy of God.

The Son of Man came eating and drinking, and they say, 'Here is a glutton and a drunkard, a friend of tax collectors and "sinners." 'But wisdom is proved right by her actions."

Matthew 11:19

This is an example of being judged by our actions. Sometimes people will draw wrong conclusions in their judgments about us. However, our consistency in a good walk with the Lord will prove them wrong.

And no wonder, for Satan himself masquerades as an angel of light. It is not surprising, then, if his servants masquerade as servants of righteousness. Their end will be what their actions deserve.

2 Corinthians 11:14-15

Our actions will reveal to whom we belong. Are we children of the light, or are we children of the darkness? Just because certain people talk and act like children of God on occasion does not mean they are of God. What is the motive behind their actions? They will be paid accordingly in the end. God will give us discernment to know when someone's actions are deceptive.

The truth of the matter is, we are responsible for our actions, regardless of others' actions and motivations. If someone is mean to us, he or she can only pull out what is in us already. We alone are responsible for our actions.

They claim to know God, but by their actions they deny him. They are detestable, disobedient and unfit for doing anything good.

Titus 1:16

We may say that we know God and claim to be Christians, but our behavior will reveal the truth.

Dear children, let us not love with words or tongue but with actions and in truth.

1 John 3:18

It is good for us to demonstrate for our children through our own actions the behavior expected of them. We must assume responsibility for our actions and provide our children with good role models. Sometimes, however, even as adults, we don't want to accept the blame for our actions. Everything is somebody else's fault: "I'm the way that I am because of my parents." "My spouse makes me act this way." "My children make me scream at them." "My job does not pay me enough money; therefore, I don't do my best at that job." But the truth is, nobody can make us do anything. We make our own choices! It is love in action when we are good examples to our children.

But I tell you that men will have to give account on the day of judgment for every careless word they have spoken. For by your words you will be acquitted, and by your words you will be condemned."

Matthew 12:36-37

As surely as I live,' says the Lord, 'every knee will bow before me; every tongue will confess to God.' 12So then, each of us will give an account of himself to God.

Romans 14:11-12

Nothing in all creation is hidden from God's sight. Everything is uncovered and laid bare before the eyes of him to whom we must give account.

Hebrews 4:13

It is good for our kids to learn to accept consequences now, because one day they will give an account to God for all their words and deeds.

Obey your leaders and submit to their authority. They keep watch over you as men who must give an account. Obey them so that their work will be a joy, not a burden, for that would be of no advantage to you.

Hebrews 13:17

Our children need to learn that their behavior can cause problems not only for them but also for those who watch over them. The people who watch over us don't generally enjoy punishing us; rather, they render correction in order to teach or eliminate certain behavior. God does not draw pleasure from disciplining us, but it is very necessary.

Pass the Blessings!

My poor children had the "pleasure" of being raised by a mother whose spiritual gift is teaching. Sometimes teachers can be so legalistic—or rather, this one was, and still is, to a certain degree. I always wanted my children to learn a lesson from the things they experienced, or sadly enough, I wanted to teach them a lesson from something they did wrong. It is true that we should learn from past mistakes, but my poor children had to hear their mistakes repeated over and over again. When they were younger, I should have loved them more in the midst of their mistakes. My oldest son received the harshest treatment because I was still learning that what I was doing was wrong. My other two children had it hard too, but I became more apologetic as I grew older and as my husband brought my behavior to my attention through his words and actions.

The word of the LORD came to me: "What do you people mean by quoting this proverb about the land of Israel: "'The fathers eat sour grapes, and the children's teeth are set on edge'? "As surely as I live, declares the Sovereign LORD, you will no longer quote this proverb in Israel. For every living soul belongs to me, the father as well as the son—both alike belong to me. The soul who sins is the one who will die. "Suppose there is a righteous man who does what is just and right. He does not eat at the mountain shrines or look to the idols of the house of Israel. He does not defile his neighbor's wife or lie with a woman during her period. He does not oppress anyone, but returns what he took in pledge for a loan. He does not commit robbery but gives his food to the hungry and provides clothing for the naked. He does not lend at usury or take excessive interest. He withholds his hand from doing wrong and judges fairly between man and man. He follows my decrees and faithfully keeps my laws. That man is righteous; he will surely live, declares the Sovereign LORD." Suppose he has a violent son, who sheds blood or does any of these other things (though the father has done none of them): "He eats at the mountain shrines. He defiles his neighbor's wife. He oppresses the poor and needy. He commits robbery. He does not return what he took in pledge. He looks to the idols. He does detestable things. He lends at usury and takes excessive interest. Will such a man live? He will not! Because he has done all these detestable things, he will surely be put to death and his blood will be on his own head. "But suppose this son has a son who sees all the sins his father commits, and though he sees them, he does not do such things: "He does not eat at the mountain shrines or look to the idols of the house of Israel. He does not defile his neighbor's wife. He does not oppress anyone or require a pledge for a loan. He does not commit robbery but gives his food to the hungry and provides clothing for the naked. He withholds his hand from sin and takes no usury or excessive interest. He keeps my laws and follows my decrees. He will not die for his father's sin; he will surely live. But his father will die for his own sin, because he practiced extortion, robbed his brother and did what was wrong among his people.

"Yet you ask, 'Why does the son not share the guilt of his father?' Since the son has done what is just and right and has been careful to keep all my decrees, he will surely live. The soul who sins is the one who will die. The son will not share the guilt of the father, nor will the father share the guilt of the son. The righteousness of the righteous man will be credited to him, and the wickedness of the wicked will be charged against him.

"But if a wicked man turns away from all the sins he has committed and keeps all my decrees and does what is just and right, he will surely live; he will not die. None of the offenses he has committed will be remembered against him. Because of the righteous things he has done, he will live. Do I take any pleasure in the death of the wicked? declares the Sovereign LORD. Rather, am I not pleased when they turn from their ways and live?

"But if a righteous man turns from his righteousness and commits sin and does the same detestable things the wicked man does, will he live? None of the righteous things he has done will be remembered. Because of the unfaithfulness he is guilty of and because of the sins he has committed, he will die. "Yet you say, 'The way of the Lord is not just.' Hear, O house of Israel: Is my way unjust? Is it not your ways that are unjust? If a righteous man turns from his righteousness and commits sin, he will die for it; because of the sin he has committed he will die. But if a wicked man turns away from the wickedness he has committed and does what is just and right, he will save his life. Because he considers all the offenses he has committed

and turns away from them, he will surely live; he will not die. Yet the house of Israel says, 'The way of the Lord is not just.' Are my ways unjust, O house of Israel? Is it not your ways that are unjust? "Therefore, O house of Israel, I will judge you, each one according to his ways, declares the Sovereign LORD. Repent! Turn away from all your offenses; then sin will not be your downfall. Rid yourselves of all the offenses you have committed, and get a new heart and a new spirit. Why will you die, O house of Israel? For I take no pleasure in the death of anyone, declares the Sovereign LORD. Repent and live!

Ezekiel 18:1-32

We live in a society where it seems normal to blame others for our behavior. Grown people blame their parents for their actions. Nobody wants to admit that at a certain age, we make our own decisions. Parents may have done things wrong when we were young, but as adults, we are free to think and act the way we choose. I know some people mentally struggle to make that transition, but we must realize it is up to us to control our lives. It may possibly require professional counseling to get to the place we need to be. Sometimes the long arm of generational behavior may not release the way it should as we enter adulthood, but nothing is impossible with God. We are more than conquerors in Christ!

DON'T AWAKEN LOVE

Three times Solomon advises not to awaken love before its time.

Daughters of Jerusalem, I charge you by the gazelles and by the does of the field: Do not arouse or awaken love.

Song of Solomon 2:7

Daughters of Jerusalem, I charge you by the gazelles and by the does of the field: Do not arouse or awaken love until it so desires.

Song of Solomon 3:5

Daughters of Jerusalem, I charge you: Do not arouse or awaken love until it so desires.

Song of Solomon 8:4

In our society today, we are not protecting our kids the way we should. We are allowing so many vile things to penetrate our kids' minds. In earlier days, movies and sitcoms would only show a man and woman in separate twin beds; now nothing is left to the imagination. Now we not only see them in the same bed, but we also see them engaged in sex acts. Furthermore, everything except the lower parts of their trunks is visible. Though I'm fifty, I blush when I see this and turn away.

Things that should lie dormant in our children are sometimes very violently awakened. Their innocence is so precious, and we should protect it any way we can. We sometimes think only babies and little children need protection, but our teens need to be protected also. There are all sorts of pedophiles who want to destroy our children's lives.

When I was growing up, a married man in the church was constantly watching me, talking to me and trying to persuade me to meet with him. He wanted to take me to school, but I don't think I would have made it there. In my innocence, I thought the attention was flattering, but to meet with him privately didn't feel right. Thank God, one of my older sisters, Jeffery, noticed what was going on and confronted the man. She told him she would inform his wife and the church of his inappropriate behavior if he didn't leave me alone. I never had any more problems with him. Thank God, someone was watching over me.

In the school I attended, it was common for boys to just reach out and grab girls. These incidents frustrated me greatly. I hated such behavior, but it happened to many of us girls. I also remember that when I was a young teen at one of my first jobs, the manager would grab the female employees' bottoms. The grown women accepted this behavior without complaining, but I thought to myself, *Is this right?* I needed to see them stand up for themselves, but since they did not, I lacked the strength to do so either. I decided not to say anything to my mother and endured the horrible behavior. I hated the feelings this created inside of me, and I did not like the women I worked with because they did nothing to stop the crude behavior. Thankfully, since the job was only a temporary job for the Christmas season, I did not have to endure the harassment for long. However, if those adult women had stood up for themselves, what power they would have given a teenage girl! Ladies, we must set good examples for young women—we don't know when they are watching us.

We are guilty, too, when we don't monitor the activity of our children on the computer or the radio, with videos and games, and concerning barbershop talk from others and ourselves. Three times Solomon cautioned against awakening love before its time. My daughter, who was between six and eight years old at the time, once clicked on a cartoon character on the computer, and some nudity appeared on the screen. This scared her, as it rightfully should have. Her innocence was under attack, and it hurt her. It hurt me, too, because I was always quite diligent about my kids' protection.

The enemy, however, is just as diligent in his attacks on our kids. Proverbs instructs us to diligently guard our minds, so that must mean they are constantly under attack. Some people think I go overboard in trying to protect my children, but it takes only one time for a child's life to be ruined. I don't mean to say that God can't heal; I'm saying we should try to prevent the events in the first place that would cause our children to need healing. We must constantly cover our children in prayer. There is a time for their bodies and minds to experience certain things, but that time is not when they are kids and teenagers. But some people will try to take advantage of their youthful innocence. My sons, when they were only teenagers, were approached by grown women. It is not just men who are predators; there are women on the prowl too.

Even parents can awaken things before their season if they behave inappropriately in front of their children. The way some people act in parks, at restaurants, and on public transportation never ceases to amaze me. In some cases, the only thing missing in their public displays of affection is the bed itself.

There is a time for everything, and a season for every activity under heaven.

Ecclesiates 3:1

Awake, north wind, and come, south wind! Blow on my garden, that its fragrance may spread abroad. Let my lover come into his garden and taste its choice fruits.

Solomon 4:16

There is a proper time for our physical bodies to awaken to the sensual desires that God put there. That's right—God put them there for a good reason. He wants a man and a woman to experience physical pleasure when they come together in marriage.

When someone awakens a child's innocence, it does not always remain a secret. These children may exhibit certain behaviors as a result of the abuse and predators recognize those signs. Kids who have been abused, therefore, are sometimes abused multiple times.

The woman in the Scripture above is inviting someone to taste her choice fruit, but some people today are picking fruit from children, and this is harmful to them. As a matter of fact, the fruit is not even ripe. It is still green, but this does not deter some from sampling the choice fruits of innocence.

He has taken me to the banquet hall, and his banner over me is love.

Solomon 2:4

In this Scripture, the woman freely expresses her love for her lover. She celebrates the fact that she treasures him, and she wants everyone to know it. True love is celebrated and openly shared with others. It is not hidden, as though it were something dirty. We must teach our kids to immediately report to family members, teachers, neighbors, or anyone who can help them with any deed that someone says must be kept secret.

I belong to my lover, and his desire is for me.

Solomon 7:10

This is especially true of those who follow the corrupt desire of the sinful nature and despise authority.

2 Peter 2:10

When we walk according to the flesh rather than according to the Spirit, there are no limits to what the flesh will do. The flesh has not been baptized in the Holy Spirit, and we cannot make ourselves the perfect people that God requires. Our fleshly nature really doesn't like laws or authorities that tell us what we can and cannot do. Our society encourages us that if something feels good, we should do it. When Nike says "Just do it!" what does that mean? We cannot leave words like these unexplained to our children.

Hold on to instruction; do not let it go; guard it well, for it is your life.

Proverbs 4:13

We must teach our children instructions from the Word of God, and they should match the instructions that we live by and give to them. We should go over our rules and the Word constantly, because the flesh won't automatically hold on to it. As matter of fact, the flesh fights it. The Old Testament says to put the Word around our necks, or as glasses before our eyes, so that we won't forget the instructions of the Lord.

Flesh gives birth to flesh, but the Spirit gives birth to spirit.

John3:6

The fact of something being awakened implies that it was present already. God made our physical bodies, and each part has a function. Some of the body parts and senses are awakened at the exact moment of their creation, while others have a later time marked for their awakening. The innocence of our children depends upon our actions to step up and protect them from premature awakenings.

There is a time for everything, and a season for every activity under heaven

Ecclesiastes 3:1

Be happy, young man, while you are young, and let your heart give you joy in the days of your youth. Follow the ways of your heart and whatever your eyes see, but know that for all these things God will bring you to judgment.

Ecclesiastes 11:9

God wants us to have fun; the youth are addressed in this verse because they live in a joyful period of life before the cares of the world press in, cares like finding a job and taking care of a family. Some people think it is not fun to be a Christian. Although there is plenty of freedom in Christ, they see only the things that they cannot do and conclude they are getting the short end of the stick. I have always had so much fun in my life as a Christian. As a young person, my faith helped me avoid making some of the poor decisions that others made, and I am happy for that. Thankfully, my mother did everything in her power to protect and cover me, including praying. I'm not saying that I did not make any mistakes as a twenty-something person; some of my biggest mistakes were made in my twenties. But I did have a foundation that provided strength and stability.

Remember your Creator in the days of your youth, before the days of trouble come and the years approach when you will say, "I find no pleasure in them

Ecclesiastes 12:1

Unless Christ intervenes, we will not find pleasure in our older days if we make poor decisions in our youth. We can help our kids so they won't have to live with the same regrets that we have. Of course, they may not heed our advice, but at least we can try to show them the way. Their fun may be sweet now, but as they become wiser, they will more clearly recognize the wrong they have done, though the consequences may always be part of their lives.

How can a young man keep his way pure? By living according to your word. [10]I seek you with all my heart; do not let me stray from your commands. [11]I have hidden your word in my heart that I might not sin against you.

Psalms 119:9-11

That is the secret to our success with temptation. Hiding the Word of God in our hearts is accomplished by reading, meditating on, and living God's Word. To live a life dedicated to the things of Christ, one must make a premeditated decision to do so. It has to be done intentionally and wholeheartedly. If the decision is not made until the heat of battle, we may not emerge unharmed. Success is more likely when we set our minds ahead of time and keep them set.

When tempted, no one should say, "God is tempting me." For God cannot be tempted by evil, nor does he tempt anyone; but each one is tempted when, by his own evil desire, he is dragged away and enticed. Then, after desire has conceived, it gives birth to sin; and sin, when it is full-grown, gives birth to death.

James1:13-15

The current generation of youth has much more to entice them than we did twenty and thirty years ago. We didn't have to worry about the Internet and its predators, immoral TV or radio programs, provocative magazines and billboards, or the behavior of people in public places. But today nothing is left to the imagination because nothing remains hidden. Some things, however, need to stay hidden. Take, for instance, the clothes offered for sale for young women. Pieces of clothing once regarded as undergarments are now worn as outer garments. Much of the clothing is sheer, low cut, too short, too tight, or emblazoned with insinuating pictures and words. Movies now rated PG and PG-13 were once rated R, until our morals began descending on a slippery slope to perversion.

As a result of all these factors, many feelings and behaviors in our children are awakened very early and very abruptly. Because they are immature, they don't know what to do with this information, but it plants itself inside their minds, and they can't erase it. I remember the first time I saw nudity in a book. I couldn't get those images out of my mind. It wasn't that I wanted to think about them; I just couldn't make them go away.

When I was a child, it wasn't the TV, radio, or the Internet that would have awakened anything sensual. It would have been an event or a person. In this day and age, our kids have to be warned of many more things than we did. There are more people assaulting their innocence in a variety of ways. The Internet can be a wonderful tool, but it can also be a dangerous one. A certain sexual, deviant crudeness has been revealed, and it is sickening.

MEN ARE NEEDED

It takes a male and a female to make a child. That should let us know that it takes two, a male and a female, to raise a child. There are issues that only a mother can address in her sons and daughters, and there are other issues that only a father can minister to in his children's lives. Society, however, has slowly gone on a rampage to devalue the role of the father. There are so many shows like *Love and Marriage, The George Lopez Show, The Bill Engvall Show,* and others where the fathers are constantly demeaned by wives, children, neighbors, and friends. There is absolutely no respect or honor shown them. I believe this is a work of the enemy, who does not want us to know we have a heavenly Father who loves us and deserves all honor and respect. He has a systematic plan to get rid of the idea that we need fathers and, by extension, our heavenly Father.

I thank God for the single mothers who are raising their children alone, but that was never God's plan. I was a single mother for a while, as was my mother and some of my sisters, nieces, cousins, and friends, so I know how difficult the job is. Even after my second marriage, there were days when I was not at my best, but I had my husband to help me. There were also days when he needed me to help him see things differently. Children need to hear the voices of both mothers and fathers and see the reasoning behind their different views.

Children will miss out if raised my two women or two men. No matter how much testosterone has been placed in a woman, she is still a woman, and no matter how much estrogen has been placed in a man, he is still a man. It doesn't matter how people dress or act; they are still the gender that God created them. I can't model for my daughter the way a man should treat her. My husband can't model for my sons how a woman should respond to a man. Additionally, there are many things that a daughter would rather not discuss with her father and many things a son would rather not discuss with his mother.

So Gideon took the men down to the water. There the Lord told him," Separate those who lap the water with their tongues like a dog from those who kneel down to drink." Three hundred men lapped with their hands to their mouth. All the rest got down on their knees to drink. The Lord said to Gideon," With the three hundred men that lapped I will save you and give the Midianites (your enemies) into your hands…

Judges 7:5 - 7a

Gideon was a fearful man, and the Lord wanted to show him that He would be with him, no matter how big the enemy. God wanted to show Gideon that it was not by his strength or might that he would conquer. It would be only by his faith in God. God instructed Gideon to choose only the men who were watchful for the enemy at all times. Those men who knelt down to drink were not watchful of what could come against them.

The man of the family is needed to be watchful for whatever may come against the family. If the woman is trying to do this, along with everything else she has to do, it is not nearly as effective. The two should work as a team with God to ward off enemy attacks. This does not mean that our families will never be attacked, but God will be with us. We are human, and we do get tired and weary. That is why it is good to have two fighting for the family; one can fight when the other is weak.

Devote yourself to prayer, being watchful and careful.

Colossians 4:2

These directives are needed in our spiritual lives, regardless of the circumstances. It is important for the head of the house to consult the Lord on things that pertain to the future and well-being of the family. The family needs his protection and coverage from the enemies of the world. Satan loves to attack the family because its success advances the kingdom and multiplies the number of those who will make a stand against the kingdom of darkness.

In the family, the man is needed to make a stand and fight along with his wife for his personal success as well as the success of his wife and children. Generally, the wife gives comfort, is the cheerleader of the family, provides taxi service, does the cooking, and makes sure the family has all those little things they don't even pay attention to on a daily basis. Things like clean clothes, towels, and washcloths are some of the overlooked items that a family enjoys.

The children are the future of the family. The enemy attacks our kids by trying to discourage them and make them fearful about the future. At such times, a father needs to be there to encourage his children and let them know that he believes in them. Though mothers are encouragers also, there is something about a male figure that helps children in ways that a mother just cannot do.

When David and his men came to Ziklag on the third day, they found it destroyed by fire and their wives and sons and daughter they had taken captive. So David and his men wept aloud until they had no strength left to weep.

1 Samuel 30:3 -4

David left to fight a fight that was not his. He was a warrior and good at it, but this particular fight was not something he needed to do. He was engaged in unnecessary work outside the home, and he also took others away from their homes, leaving at risk all their homes, wives, and children. As a result, David's family was taken away, and he had to fight to get them back.

But keep in mind, David would not have had to fight for his family if he had been prayerful and watchful in the first place. However, God did restore David's family and possessions to him. He didn't suffer loss, because he acted quickly when he talked with the Lord and received word to go. God loved David, but He loves all men just as much. He will help them with their families and tell them which tools of warfare to use. The main weapons, of course, are the Word of God and prayer.

It is the nature of most men to work and take care of a home, whether an individual home or one they share with a wife and children. Some men, however, are workaholics and don't spend enough time at home helping their wives with everything involved in maintaining a successful family. Some like hanging out with the guys, while others give more time to church than to their families, though that is not God's will. Some men want only to sit in front of the television, forgetting that their wives need their help. And then there are some who refuse to step up to the plate and help with the discipline and guidance of their children; they only want to have fun with them.

Under three things the earth trembles, under four it cannot bear up. An unloved woman who is married.

Proverbs 30:21

If a woman is married, she should be loved and sense that love. If not, then what is the sense in her being married? She could just as easily remain single and not feel loved. She will, however, always be loved by the Father.

When a man is single, he is allowed to spend time with his male friends in good, clean, appropriate fun. When he marries, things should change. Yes, he can still spend time with his friends, but there should be a change in both quantity and priority of time spent with them.

When children are brought into the family, they need to feel loved also. The mother can't always give effectively what she does not receive. Good men are needed to fill this role in their families. Their wives need their help with the kids, the house, and everything else necessary for a good Christian family. This is so important that the book of Proverbs says the earth trembles and cannot bear up under the effects of an unloved married woman. That is a deep statement.

For this reason a man shall leave his father and mother and be united to his wife, and the two shall become one flesh.

Genesis 2:24

If a man is instructed to leave his father and mother, then this principle certainly applies to his friends. Again, that does not mean he must abandon these relationships, only that his wife and family should take precedence. I firmly believe in men bonding with other men. I know I place great importance on my relationships with several groups of women in my life, and I want my husband to have that with the male friends in his life. My husband's best friend has been in his life since he was three or four years old, and it is good for them to spend time together.

Similarly, encourage the young men to be self-controlled. In everything set them an example by doing what is good. In your teaching show integrity, seriousness and soundness of speech that cannot be condemned, so that those who oppose you may be ashamed because they have nothing bad to say about us.

Titus 2:6-8

Men are needed to encourage and set examples for their sons and other young men. This is so important because a woman or mother cannot teach a boy or young man how to be a man and act like a man. I know this was mentioned in a previous chapter, but it so important to say it again.

Boys need men to show them how to work and take care of the family. Statistics show that 70 to 75 percent of all people in jail did not have fathers in their lives. This sad and stunning fact should make men realize the importance of being a part of their children's lives.

A father's presence is just as important to a daughter's life as to a son's. I have never in my life been able to call anybody Dad or Daddy. To this day, there remains a sore spot in my heart because of that loss. As I watch my husband and daughter, I long to have experienced that kind of relationship.

A man needs to know that his wife is capable of taking care of the family in his absence, but she should not have to do this on a regular basis. His presence should be sorely missed when he is gone. Though I am thankful for my heavenly Father, He set it up so that women and children need the presence of men in their lives. We need fathers, husbands, and grandfathers to show us what true godly males should look like. Good male mentors are desperately needed to fill this void.

Only God our Father can play all roles in our lives. He is called El Shaddai, which means "the breasted one." He nurtures us and provides us with the life-sustaining substance that we need. He is our all, and we can find all in Him. That is the comfort for those like me who have never had fathers in their lives.

You are witnesses, and so is God, of how holy, righteous and blameless we were among you who believed. For you know that we dealt with each of you as a father deals with his own children, encouraging, comforting and urging you to live lives worthy of God, who calls you into his kingdom and glory.

1 Thessalonians 2:10-12

A GOOD MOTHER

I have been reminded of your sincere faith, which first lived in your grandmother Lois and in your mother Eunice and, I am persuaded, now lives in you also.

2 Timothy 1:5

Timothy had a grandmother who loved God and lived according to His Word. She taught her daughter the ways of the Lord and lived a righteous life before her. These two women in turn taught and modeled Christ before Timothy. Our children will learn our ways and the actions we model before them. We can teach them at an early age to be followers of Christ. Our children should grow in the shadow of generational love and examples.

Saul's anger flared up at Jonathan and he said to him, "You son of a perverse and rebellious woman! Don't I know that you have sided with the son of Jesse to your own shame and to the shame of the mother who bore you?

1 Samuel 20:30

Whatever a child's actions, they reflect the type of home the child was raised in. The child's actions, good or bad, reflect the parents' influence. Saul immediately labeled Jonathan's mother's character as perverse and rebellious and said that Jonathan was behaving just like her.

The next mother taught her son to be like her, whether she intended to or not. She involved him in her conniving, stealing, lying ways, and as he watched her, he learned her ways well.

Now Rebekah was listening as Isaac spoke to his son Esau. When Esau left for the open country to hunt game and bring it back, Rebekah said to her son Jacob, "Look, I overheard your father say to your brother Esau, Bring me some game and prepare me some tasty food to eat, so that I may give you my blessing in the presence of the LORD before I die.' Now, my son, listen carefully and do what I tell you: Go out to the flock and bring me two choice young goats, so I can prepare some tasty food for your father, just the way he likes it. Then take it to your father to eat, so that he may give you his blessing before he dies."

Genesis 27:5-10

Jacob grew up to be like his mother, who was a trickster and a con artist. Unfortunately, Jacob received the same type of treatment as he gave; he reaped the seeds that he had sowed. His own father-in-law tricked him into working seven years for the daughter that Jacob wanted, but on the wedding night, Jacob was given a different daughter. He felt deceived, as he should have, but now he knew how it must have felt when he tricked others. He had to work another seven years for the daughter he wanted to marry. The entire chronicle of events can be found in Genesis 29 and 30.

But Samuel was ministering before the LORD—a boy wearing a linen ephod. Each year his mother made him a little robe and took it to him when she went up with her husband to offer the annual sacrifice

1 Samuel 2: 18-19

Hannah gave Samuel back to the Lord for service in the temple. She provided for him by making him a linen ephod. The process by which linen was made was not an easy one. Made from flax, the plant had to be gathered and then taken through a certain process. Hannah recognized Samuel's needs and ministered to them.

When Bathsheba went to King Solomon to speak to him for Adonijah, the king stood up to meet her, bowed down to her and sat down on his throne. He had a throne brought for the king's mother, and she sat down at his right hand.

1 Kings 2:19

King Solomon had such respect, honor, and love for his mother. He stood up when she entered the room, and he even set up a throne near him to show the depth of his feelings for her. I believe he poured this love back into his mother because she had poured it into him. You cannot give what you don't have. Bathsheba had done much right in the life of Solomon; however, we should not forget David's contributions.

The rod of correction imparts wisdom, but a child left to himself disgraces his mother.

Proverbs 29:15

The use of the rod implies that we will do whatever it takes to correct our children. We may or may not have to go in that particular path. However, when children are permitted to do as they please and are not corrected when they do wrong, they shame their mothers by their behavior. Our children have enough friends—they need parents. In many instances, there is only a mother or grandmother taking care of the child. Sometimes there is only a father or grandfather; even in these instances, mothering and nurturing, though difficult for men, are not impossible. With God, all things are possible.

She speaks with wisdom, and faithful instruction is on her tongue.

Proverbs 31:26

If we are to speak wisdom, we have to take measures to attain it inside of us. Age does not automatically bring wisdom, for there are many adults who are not wise. If we want wisdom, we have to set aside time to read God's Word, pray and meditate on what it says, and then actually live it out in front of our children. We can then share with our children the wisdom we have learned from the Word and from our life experiences.

If a man curses his father or mother, his lamp will be snuffed out in pitch darkness.

Proverbs 20:20

Honor and respect for parents is high on God's list of required behavior. In fact, it is one of the Ten Commandments. The Word says that a child's life is lengthened by his or her obedience. Again, we can help our children by not letting them get away with behavior that is not profitable to their lives. For example, we should never allow children to talk back and show disrespect for any reason.

I've heard some parents say, "I want to raise my children to speak up for themselves and speak their minds." Well, I work in a middle school, and let me tell you, this mind-set only brings forth out-of-control teens. These young people think they are right in many instances, even though they have very limited information and experience on which to base their decisions.

I once witnessed a student stand up and mouth off to the principal at my school. I was not happy about this because I knew of no other principal who cared as deeply for the well-being of her students as did Mrs. Williams. She often brought struggling students into her office to read with them and help them any way she could, only to sometimes have these very same students be disrespectful later on. If children will curse their mothers or fathers, then they will curse and disrespect any other adult. Come on, mothers, let's help our children to be respectful, and let's show them diplomatic ways to talk to and reason with adults.

As a mother comforts her child, so will I comfort you; and you will be comforted over Jerusalem."

Isaiah 66:13

A mother comforts! In the verse above, God compared a mother's comfort to the comfort that He wanted to give Jerusalem. The word *comfort* means to encourage or give a sense of ease to someone, or to help make life easier. It means to provide a state of quiet enjoyment! We do this for our children by providing them with quiet homes as places of refuge from the cares of life. They do have reasonable and true cares in their lives; they might be different from our cares, but, nevertheless, very real to them.

Normally, I speak with a higher tone than do most people. When I get excited, my voice goes even higher. Also, my spiritual gift is teaching, which can be good or bad for the people around me. Unless controlled by the Holy Spirit, a teacher is always in the learning and teaching-a-lesson mode. My poor children were always being taught a lesson. Sometimes I was so legalistic with them, but I have improved with age. I was not the "huggy feely" type of mother, but I did try to comfort my children and spend plenty of time with them. I did provide them with a sense of protection and enjoyment, and I loved creating good memories in their childhood and teenage years.

Everyone who quotes proverbs will quote this proverb about you: "Like mother, like daughter." You are a true daughter of your mother, who despised her husband and her children; and you are a true sister of your sisters, who despised their husbands and their children. Your mother was a Hittite and your father an Amorite.

Ezekiel 16:44-45

It is not good, mothers, when we teach our children our bad habits and ways. Sometimes we don't realize this is happening, but we must remember they are always watching us. Mouthy mothers produce mouthy children; lying mothers, lying children; shoplifting mothers, shoplifting children. There are mothers who turn their heads when they see their children doing wrong; to their shame, they don't correct them. It is easier to let children do whatever they want than to consistently show them what they should do until they learn that lesson. In the end, all of effort will be worthwhile.

The wise woman builds her house, but with her own hands the foolish one tear hers down.

Proverbs 14:1

This Scripture speaks clearly on its own. *To build* means to increase in amount, to make desirable or attractive, to cause to be or grow, or to create or develop. Clearly, if the wise woman does these things, then the foolish woman does the opposite. Only a fool would cause her house to decrease in quality or become undesirable for her family.

There is a saying that says, "If Mama ain't happy, then nobody's happy." When I first heard these words, I laughed, but once I really thought about it, I was ashamed because it was true in my life. When I was unhappy, my home wasn't the best place to be for either my husband or my kids. But on the other hand, when I was happy, I could make things so good.

As I look back, I am so ashamed. It wasn't intentional, but the fact is, the saying was true for my house and probably is for many other women's homes as well. We women wield a power in our homes that we should use wisely. We have the power to build up and the power to tear down. We need to use that ability wisely. We will have to stand before God for our use and misuse of our position in the home.

INTERCESSION—BUILD A WALL

Pray for your children without ceasing!

Because a great door for effective work has opened to me, and there are many who oppose me.

1 Corinthians 16:9

Whenever there are opportunities for our kids to advance, the enemy is there to throw roadblocks in their way.

Be self-controlled and alert. Your enemy the devil prowls around like a roaring lion looking for someone to devour.

1 Peter 5:8

When something is devoured, it is destroyed. It does not benefit the enemy and his evil plan for our kids to grow up confident and successful. There are so many negative things that come at them, seeking to distract them from God's plans for their lives. We have to be diligent to assist our kids in prayer and with knowledge, being available to them in times of need. They do need independence, but they need guidance also, just as we need guidance and help at our age.

I urge, then, first of all, that requests, prayers, intercession and thanksgiving be made for everyone.

1 Timothy 2:1

...a man whose name was Job. This man was blameless and upright; he feared God and shunned evil. He had seven sons and three daughters, His sons used to take turns holding feasts in their homes, and they would invite their three sisters to eat and drink with them. When a period of feasting had run its course, Job would send and have them purified. Early in the morning he would sacrifice a burnt offering for each of them, thinking, "Perhaps my children have sinned and cursed God in their hearts." This was Job's regular custom

Job 1:1-2 & 4-5

Job was a good and righteous man, and he knew he had taught his children the ways of the Lord. However, even though we may teach our children right, they sometimes do things contrary to the way we have taught them.

The children gather wood, the fathers light the fire, and the women knead the dough and make cakes of bread for the Queen of Heaven. They pour out drink offerings to other gods to provoke me to anger. But am I the one they are provoking? declares the LORD. Are they not rather harming themselves, to their own shame?

Jeremiah 7:18-19

We have to be careful of the activities that we involve our children in, because not only do we make them vulnerable to the consequences of the activities at that time, but we also open the door for them to choose those activities later in life. By our neglect, we can open the door and show them the way down a wrong path. We can better negotiate inappropriate behavior if we are not responsible for having started it in the first place.

Do not be anxious about anything, but in everything, by prayer and petition, with thanksgiving, present your requests to God.

Phillipians 4:6

God does know everything; however, we are to go to Him with everything that is on our hearts. With no anxiety, we can talk to Him and thank Him for listening and answering us with His infinite knowledge. He loves our children more than we do; He created them and had a plan for their lives long before we even thought of them.

"Have you not put a hedge around him and his household and everything he has? You have blessed the work of his hands, so that his flocks and herds are spread throughout the land.

Job 1:10

The same hedge that God placed around Job can be placed around our children. God protected Job and his children and caused them to prosper. Although the enemy wanted to get in, he could not, until he received permission. Even when the enemy was allowed entrance, God knew that Job could bear up under it, because He will not allow us to be tried beyond what we can bear.

No temptation has seized you except what is common to man. And God is faithful; he will not let you be tempted beyond what you can bear. But when you are tempted, he will also provide a way out so that you can stand up under it.

1 Corinthians 10:13

Our children will face consequences for their actions, but it will never be more than they can bear. God is all about our success, but there will be times when we must receive punishment. We should encourage our children and pray for them as they go through their difficulties. We should pray continuously for them!

Carry each other's burdens, and in this way you will fulfill the law of Christ.

Galatians 6:2

In praying with them and for them, we help to carry their burdens. We can read Scripture to them to show them the might and power of God. Sometimes we may even need to fast and pray for our children.

Jesus replied, "And you experts in the law, woe to you, because you load people down with burdens they can hardly carry, and you yourselves will not lift one finger to help them.

Luke 11:46

Unfortunately, sometimes we place burdens on our children that we ourselves could not bear. Not everything that our parents did to us is good for our children. Certain things they did when we were kids may not have seemed harsh to us, but those very same things may seem harsh to our children. We are all individuals, and it will take guidance from the Lord to know what is good for a particular child and specific situation.

Cain said to the LORD, "My punishment is more than I can bear. Today you are driving me from the land, and I will be hidden from your presence; I will be a restless wanderer on the earth, and whoever finds me will kill me." But the LORD said to him, "Not so; if anyone kills Cain, he will suffer vengeance seven times over." Then the LORD put a mark on Cain so that no one who found him would kill him.

Genesis 4:13-15

Although our children will have to suffer the consequences for their wrong actions, God still does not abandon them. He still protects and cares for them if, like Cain, they ask for His help. We should also pray and make petitions with thanksgiving. We must thank God always because it could always be worse.

But let all who take refuge in you be glad; let them ever sing for joy. Spread your protection over them, that those who love your name may rejoice in you. 12For surely, O LORD, you bless the righteous; you surround them with your favor as with a shield.

Psalms 5:11-12

If we truly love the Lord, He will make things work for our good. We will receive His favor and blessings as a shield around us. A shield is used to protect us from something harmful directed towards us. God is our shield!

My shield is God Most High, who saves the upright in heart.

Psalms 7:10

(Love)*It always protects.*

1 Corinthians 13:7

Love always protects! God loves us, and we love our children. It should always reside in us to protect our children. Interceding before God for them is a true way to love them.

Therefore I will block her path with thorn bushes; I will wall her in so that she cannot find her way. She will chase after her lovers but not catch them; she will look for them but not find them.

Hosea 2:6-7

Hosea was married to a prostitute who would leave him at times to return to her old ways. He knew the strong pull on her to return to that life. There are things in our children's lives that have a strong pull on them. We may have experienced the same things and conquered them quite easily, but that may not be the case for our children. However, we can pray and ask God to show us ways to block them from succeeding in returning to their old ways. They may even fight against us, but we must still be diligent in helping them in their weakness. Sometimes drastic events call for drastic measures.

I have given them your word and the world has hated them, for they are not of the world any more than I am of the world. My prayer is not that you take them out of the world but that you protect them from the evil one. They are not of the world, even as I am not of it. Sanctify them by the truth; your word is truth. As you sent me into the world, I have sent them into the world.

John 17:14-18

God's Word sanctifies us and sets us apart from the world; therefore, we should teach our children God's Word and help them to memorize Scripture. Our children won't be taken out of the world, but they can be protected from the evil one. Because they are not of this world, they won't always be liked, and we should warn them of this fact. It is so important for teens to be liked by their peers that sometimes they are tempted to do things contrary to God's Word. Just as Jesus prayed for His disciples and for us in this Scripture, we should pray and intercede for our children.

I have to admit that most teens resent it when their parents try to protect them. They think nothing bad will happen to them—only to everyone else. They think they will never get in an accident or be abused in any way. They don't think they could possibly be abducted, and some even think they can keep drug and alcohol use as recreational without ever becoming addicted.

If only they could learn from the guidance of parents, relatives, teachers, preachers, and others. If only they could listen to people who have gone down the same road they are traveling. But too often they think they are smarter and will not make the same mistakes as others. True, that is possible, but they still need to know what to expect if they take certain paths.

SPOKEN WORDS

He appointed military officers over the people and assembled them before him in the square at the city gate and encouraged them with these words: "Be strong and courageous. Do not be afraid or discouraged because of the king of Assyria and the vast army with him, for there is a greater power with us than with him. With him is only the arm of flesh, but with us is the LORD our God to help us and to fight our battles." And the people gained confidence from what Hezekiah the king of Judah said.

2 Chronicles 32:6-8

Just as Hezekiah encouraged his men before going into battle, we must encourage our children because life is a battle. Being a child or teenager is more difficult today than it was when I was young. Peer pressure and cliques exclude some children from being part of certain groups. Trying to keep up with others to prove their worth is something many teens face daily. Encouraging them and giving them confidence to be themselves are what our children need from us as parents and teachers. As Christians, we do indeed occupy a better position, as explained in the Bible, and we must teach that to our children.

"If someone ventures a word with you, will you be impatient? But who can keep from speaking? Think how you have instructed many, how you have strengthened feeble hands. Your words have supported those who stumbled; you have strengthened faltering knees.

Job 4:2-4

It is good for us to make time to talk with our kids when they need to talk. If the thought is urgent to them but we don't make time, the opportunity may be lost forever. We have to be patient with them about whatever they are trying to share and help them when they feel weak and want to give up. I know I did not do well plenty of times in the past. I have tried to do better, and now I do stop and make eye contact to show my children that I am listening and concerned. Just as we listen and offer encouragement to friends or coworkers, we should do the same with our children.

Reckless words pierce like a sword, but the tongue of the wise brings healing.

Proverbs 12:18

The tongue that brings healing is a tree of life, but a deceitful tongue crushes the spirit.

Proverbs 15:4

When we speak to people without thinking, we can do a lot of damage. There is an old saying that goes, "Sticks and stones may break my bones, but words will never hurt me." However, this is not true, because words can and do hurt us. Once they have come out of the mouth, the damage is done. Although we may say we're sorry, the words are not forgotten.

Reckless words pierce like a sword. Statements like "you're always doing things wrong" can make a child stop trying and lose confidence. If better words are chosen, such as "you'll do better next time; I believe in you," a child can find the perseverance to conquer the problem. We do much damage to the spirit by speaking the wrong words.

The tongue has the power of life and death, and those who love it will eat its fruit.

Proverbs 18:21

This is very powerful Scripture! Knowing that we can bring life or death to someone with our words should cause all of us to think before speaking. Sadly, I used to pride myself on the fact that I could bring people down with my sarcasm and cruel words. It was something that I had mastered well. I proudly spoke without thinking, but that is the sign of a fool. May God forgive me for the damage that I did. Unfortunately, I wielded a double-edged sword. I could also give a look that made a person feel like nothing. To my discredit, I was proud of this. I loved the ability to bring somebody down to a lower level. The sad part about this is that I knew how it felt to receive these actions, but still I did them to others. Why? I can't and don't blame anyone but me.

She speaks with wisdom, and faithful instruction is on her tongue.

Proverbs 31:26

A godly woman speaks with wisdom that she has gained from studying the Word and spending time with the Lord. She knows that it is not her knowledge and plan that are needed to raise her children, but God's. She faithfully instructs her children so that they can succeed. She wants what is best for them, as does their father.

A fool's talk brings a rod to his back, but the lips of the wise protect them.

Proverbs 14:3

This saying is not just for the young; it also applies to foolish parents who instruct their children unwisely and with selfish motives. Such instruction harms children, but the wisdom of a parent who listens to the Word of the Lord will help them to make good decisions. It will be their protection in life's circumstances. There will be times when they will go through trials, but they will not be alone, for God will always stand behind His Word.

The wise in heart are called discerning, and pleasant words promote instruction.

Proverbs 16:21

Those people who have the Word stored in them are able to give good advice and speak the truth in a tone that is palatable to the hearer. The hearer will give more thought to what is said simply because harsh words and tones were not used.

The mouth of the righteous is a fountain of life, but violence overwhelms the mouth of the wicked.

Proverbs 10:11

If accepted, good words spoken to encourage others or even to correct them will add life. The choice is up to the hearer. It is not wise to listen to or follow the advice of an unwise person.

With his mouth the godless destroys his neighbor, but through knowledge the righteous escape.

Proverbs 11:9

Our mouths can do so much damage! We can destroy the lives of the people closest to us, the very ones we should be protecting. Just as our families need our protection, our neighbors need it too. Remember, the Scripture says to love your neighbor as yourself. Life and death are in the tongue.

The words of the wicked lie in wait for blood, but the speech of the upright rescues them.

Proverbs 12:6

All of these Scriptures show us the harm that our mouths can do. A person does not have to hear the actual words come out of our mouths. We set things in motion when we utter words that speak death, but we also have the power to speak words that bring life.

Hope deferred makes the heart sick, but a longing fulfilled is a tree of life.

Proverbs 13:12

Do our children hope to hear words of affirmation from us? Hope is not usually a hidden thing. We can generally tell what a person needs, but will we open up and give it? He who knows to do right and does not do it, to him it is sin.

Jesus called the crowd to him and said, "Listen and understand. What goes into a man's mouth does not make him 'unclean,' but what comes out of his mouth, that is what makes him 'unclean.'

Matthews 15:10&11

You brood of vipers, how can you who are evil say anything good? For out of the overflow of the heart the mouth speaks. The good man brings good things out of the good stored up in him, and the evil man brings evil things out of the evil stored up in him. But I tell you that men will have to give account on the day of judgment for every careless word they have spoken. For by your words you will be acquitted, and by your words you will be condemned."

Matthew 12: 34-37

The good man brings good things out of the good stored up in his heart, and the evil man brings evil things out of the evil stored up in his heart. For out of the overflow of his heart his mouth speaks.

Luke 6:45

These three Scriptures contain a significant message within them. Some of us can be so careful to eat the right things in order to maintain good health, but this first verse tells us that it is not what goes into us that make us unclean.

Both Matthew and Luke apparently saw the need to include this verse. Overflowing happens when we fill something beyond its capacity; it is more than full and has a surplus of the contents. The contents overflow from the vessel onto the actual container and anything else nearby. Whatever is now on the vessel is a direct result of whatever was in the vessel to begin with.

In a similar fashion, our mouths reveal our hearts. Sometimes we say something and wonder where it came from, but the fact is, it came from somewhere in our inner being. It was there all the time; it just finally made its way to the surface. Then it overflowed and made the vessel unclean. The worst part about this is that our overflow can damage vessels or persons who are near and dear to us. Those vessels could be our children or other youth.

Instead, we must concentrate on the Word of God and spill out His goodness on our children with words of encouragement, hope, instruction, and discipline. We have to imagine their vessels as empty and remember that every time we open our mouths, we fill them up with whatever we say. We cannot fill them up with put-downs and sarcasm and expect them to succeed and be productive.

Gold there is, and rubies in abundance, but lips that speak knowledge are a rare jewel.

Proverbs 20:15

The words that come out of our mouths are very valuable to us and to others. If we think of our words as fertilizer, food, or even weed killer for the souls of others, then maybe, under the guidance of the Holy Spirit, we will watch what we say. Certainly, in the case of children and teenagers, they need us to fill them up and give them hope for life.

WHEN BAD seems GOOD and Good seems Bad

There is a way that seems right to a man, but in the end it leads to death.

Proverbs 14:12

There is a way that seems right to a man, but in the end it leads to death.

Proverbs 16:25

All a man's ways seem innocent to him, but motives are weighed by the LORD.

Proverbs 16:2

All a man's ways seem right to him, but the LORD weighs the heart.

Proverbs 21:2

We think we are so smart! Some of us even think we are smarter than God. With our finite minds and limited knowledge, we think we know best for our lives and for others. Most of the time, we think a thing is right if the majority of people do it. We think it is right if it goes through without any problems. We think it is right if it makes us feel warm and fuzzy inside.

Unfortunately, this is not true. Many of the world's ways are not God's ways. It will not always feel good to do the right thing, nor will we always have people patting us on the back. We are in the world, but not of this world. Sometimes we do things simply because they were done in our families. Sometimes we do things because we honestly think they are right to do. Thankfully, God knows our hearts and our intentions. He knows if we are operating in ignorance or self-righteousness, and we will be judged accordingly.

The way of a fool seems right to him, but a wise man listens to advice. A fool shows his annoyance at once, but a prudent man overlooks an insult.

Proverbs 12:15-16

It is good to seek advice from wise, godly people. It is also good to move slowly and speak slowly when making decisions. It is good to teach our children not to react in anger to situations. We need time to think the issue over and pray about it. It may seem right and feel right to vent and retaliate quickly, but although we may later regret it, the damage has already been done.

The first to present his case seems right, till another comes forward and questions him.

Proverbs 18:17

For it seems to me that God has put us apostles on display at the end of the procession, like men condemned to die in the arena. We have been made a spectacle to the whole universe, to angels as well as to men. We are fools for Christ, but you are so wise in Christ! We are weak, but you are strong! You are honored, we are dishonored! To this very hour we go hungry and thirsty, we are in rags, we are brutally treated, we are homeless. We work hard with our own hands. When we are cursed, we bless; when we are persecuted, we endure it; when we are slandered, we answer kindly. Up to this moment we have become the scum of the earth, the refuse of the world.

1 Corinth 4:9-13

Doing the right thing is not always the popular thing, and sometimes we will be treated harshly for doing right. It may seem that we are not being treated fairly, but what is fair? Jesus came to save us all and make it possible for us to be with Him in heaven. In the process, He was treated harshly, but He endured it all for our sakes. At times our children will have to make unpopular stands, but they will not be alone if they are doing the will of God.

Our fathers disciplined us for a little while as they thought best; but God disciplines us for our good, that we may share in his holiness. No discipline seems pleasant at the time, but painful. Later on, however, it produces a harvest of righteousness and peace for those who have been trained by it.

Hebrews 12:10-11

The harshness and pain that we go through at times may seem unfair to us as Christians. Life is not always easy for us here on this earth, nor is it supposed to be. On this earthly journey, we receive discipline from both our earthly parents and our heavenly Father. As earthly parents, we do not have the insight of God the Father. We discipline as we think best, but God disciplines as He knows best. When we discipline our children, it will not be pleasant at the time, but it is for their good.

Beware of turning to evil, which you seem to prefer to affliction. "God is exalted in his power. Who is a teacher like him? Who has prescribed his ways for him, or said to him, 'You have done wrong'?

Job 36:21-23

We cannot turn to evil when it seems that what we perceive as right isn't working or bringing the result we want. Father God knows best, and no one can give Him counsel! No one can say, "You have messed this up, God." That is impossible. God knows all, and He knows best!

Now we pray to God that you will not do anything wrong. Not that people will see that we have stood the test but that you will do what is right even though we may seem to have failed.

2 Corinthians 13: 7

When everything around us says that we have failed, we must put our trust in God that He works all things out for our good. When we are uncertain about anything, we should seek God and His righteousness first, and all other things will be taken care of.

But seek first his kingdom and his righteousness, and all these things will be given to you as well. Therefore do not worry about tomorrow, for tomorrow will worry about itself. Each day has enough trouble of its own

Matthew 6:33-34

There is so much in our world today that is bad, but because it is so common, it seems right. However, just because everyone else is doing something does not mean it is right. Just because someone pitches a fit and gets mad because we don't accept his or her ways does not mean that person is right. As a matter of fact, even if we change our minds and say the person is right, that does not mean he or she is right in the sight of God.

Being politically correct is important to many people today. To be politically correct, a person must agree with the world and what it says is right. Far too many people value what other people say is right rather than what God says is right. As Christians, we may stand out from the rest of society, and we will probably be ostracized at times, but the Scripture says if the world loves us and agrees with us, then there is a problem. We have to be in the world, but not of the world.

When my kids were picked on by other kids, it seemed good to tell them to punch the other kids' lights out. Why? Because I wanted them to learn to protect themselves. It seems good to never again loan someone money if that person doesn't repay you the first time. It seems good to take back your coat from someone who has taken yours. But in all these cases, there are Scriptures to the contrary. Situations are so much better when we allow God to intervene.

FORSAKEN—PARENTS OUT OF LIFE

"You believe at last!" Jesus answered. "But a time is coming, and has come, when you will be scattered, each to his own home. You will leave me all alone. Yet I am not alone, for my Father is with me. "I have told you these things, so that in me you may have peace. In this world you will have trouble. But take heart! I have overcome the world."

John 16:31-33

Jesus was abandoned by earthly family and friends when He needed them most. He was also separated from His heavenly Father. His enemies put Him to death for no reason. He can identify with our alone times. He knows how it feels to be deserted.

From the sixth hour until the ninth hour darkness came over all the land. About the ninth hour Jesus cried out in a loud voice, "Eloi, Eloi, lama sabachthani?"—which means, "My God, my God, why have you forsaken me?"

Matthews 27:45-46

My God, my God, why have you forsaken me? Why are you so far from saving me, so far from the words of my groaning? O my God, I cry out by day, but you do not answer, by night, and am not silent. Yet you brought me out of the womb; you made me trust in you even at my mother's breast. From birth I was cast upon you; from my mother's womb you have been my God. Do not be far from me, for trouble is near and there is no one to help.

Psalms 22:1-2,9-11

David also felt forsaken by God. He felt that God was so far from him that He didn't even hear his prayers. On the cross, Jesus, too, felt forsaken by God. His human side begged God to save Him, while His God side knew what must be done for our sakes. He chose to endure the cross so that we could know and feel His presence, even when it doesn't seem true.

Jesus' cry of abandonment was very real. At the time He uttered the cry, He took on the weight of the entire world's sin. God, who cannot tolerate sin, had not left Him totally, but I'm sure it felt like it.

Pass the Blessings!

I will not leave you as orphans; I will come to you. Before long, the world will not see me anymore, but you will see me. Because I live, you also will live. On that day you will realize that I am in my Father, and you are in me, I and I am in you.

John 14:18-20

I have never met my earthly father. I have never had a replacement figure to refer to as a father. I have never used or spoken the word *father* to anyone on this earth. God has always and forever been my only father. Growing up, I often felt fatherless as I watched other kids with their fathers. Yes, it was hard at times, but I did learn to trust God and to talk to Him from a very early age. There were times when His presence was so near to me that I could feel it. I knew I was not alone.

For the LORD your God is a merciful God; he will not abandon or destroy you or forget the covenant with your forefathers, which he confirmed to them by oath.

Deuteronomy 4:31

God sees everything that goes on with us.

The LORD will fulfill his purpose for me; your love, O LORD, endures forever— do not abandon the works of your hands.

Psalms 138:8

Before we ever came forth from our mothers' wombs, God had a plan for our lives. Nothing done in this life can stop that plan except us. God will not abandon us.

Though my father and mother forsake me, the LORD will receive me.

Psalms 27:10

We are hard pressed on every side, but not crushed; perplexed, but not in despair; persecuted, but not abandoned; struck down, but not destroyed. We always carry around in our body the death of Jesus, so that the life of Jesus may also be revealed in our body.

2 Corinthians 4:8-10

We can be abandoned by the ones who are supposed to protect us, but the Lord will receive us. Life will be harder for some people than for others. That's unfortunate, but they are not alone. Whatever is physical is temporary, and whatever is spiritual is eternal. Being without one or both parents is difficult on kids. It is also difficult for the parents who have to raise their children alone. But on this earth, we are not home, and not everything will be perfect here and now. People will make choices that have devastating effects on the lives of those closest to them.

Some kids are not forsaken in the sense of a parent not being there, but they are forsaken by neglect or abuse from the parent or parents. In those cases, the kids still have a feeling of aloneness because they are deprived of the love and protection, the nurturing and comfort, they should receive from watchful, caring parents. Sometimes this happens because their guardians are preoccupied with work, play, or other things, or, sadly, just not interested, though physically present. How very unfortunate! This leads to our next chapter, which is about spending time with our children.

Spending Time

It is very important to spend time with our children, even after they become teenagers. It may seem as if they don't want to be bothered with us, but that is not really true. Many times my oldest son and daughter seemed embarrassed when my husband and I chaperoned trips, taught their classes, or made them play games or watch movies with us. But as children grow older, they will recall the memories of their parents being there. It is also important for siblings to spend time with one another.

A sluggard does not plow in season; so at harvest time he looks but finds nothing.

Proverbs 20:4

We cannot be lazy about this precious time in our children's lives. It will not last forever, and the tide will soon change. So invest now in your children's lives. There will come a time when you will want them to spend time with you, but if you have not planted that seed when they were young, you will not reap a harvest when they are older.

Be devoted to one another in brotherly love. Honor one another above yourselves. Never be lacking in zeal, but keep your spiritual fervor, serving the Lord. Be joyful in hope, patient in affliction, faithful in prayer. Share with God's people who are in need. Practice hospitality.

Romans 12-10-13

This Scripture tells us to be devoted to, or spend time with, others in a loving way. To be devoted to someone is to want to spend time with that person, to give one's undivided attention. Even if we don't feel like it at the moment, others may need us at critical times in their lives that could determine the paths they choose. We need to be there especially for our children. There is not a scheduled time when things happen and they ask for our guidance or attention. At any moment, they may just need someone to listen to them. When those times arise, we should show them we love and care about them.

O LORD, what is man that you care for him, the son of man that you think of him?

Psalms 144:3

God loves us, and He takes care of us. We are the apple of His eye. He doesn't get tired, nor does He want time just for Himself. *God so loved the world that He gave.* When we have the love of God, we give. We give even when it hurts. Our children need us more than they need all the extra things we work so hard and long to provide for them.

The word of the LORD came to me: "Son of man, prophesy against the shepherds of Israel; prophesy and say to them: 'This is what the Sovereign LORD says: Woe to the shepherds of Israel who only take care of themselves! Should not shepherds take care of the flock? You eat the curds, clothe yourselves with the wool and slaughter the choice animals, but you do not take care of the flock. You have not strengthened the weak or healed the sick or bound up the injured. You have not brought back the strays or searched for the lost. You have ruled them harshly and brutally. So they were scattered because there was no shepherd, and when they were scattered they became food for all the wild animals. My sheep wandered over all the mountains and on every high hill. They were scattered over the whole earth, and no one searched or looked for them.

Ezekiel 34:1-6

Just as shepherds take care of their flocks, we should take care of our children. We didn't have them just to receive tax deductions or have live-in babysitters and maids. Nor did we have them to just let them raise themselves. Our flocks are hurting and need our attention; they can lose their way if we are not there to help them. As parents, we can be harsh at times, sometimes intentionally, but other times unintentionally because we are only doing what was passed on to us. However, as adults, we are to make changes and correct the things that we know didn't work for us or made us feel sad.

We can chase our children away in their spirits even though they are living in the house with us. We must go after them because many people and things are lying in wait for them. We may or may not get them back, but we must try. We must lay down our pride and recognize when our children are at a fork in the road where they could go either way. So many youth today have lost their way and can't find their way back. They may think they will not be allowed back, or it will be the same old way when they return. Regardless of the specific circumstance, we adults must go after them.

Three days after Christmas, I once lost one of the diamonds in my wedding ring. When I noticed it was gone, I went crazy. I backtracked everywhere that I had been, but I still could not find it. I was sick! As I stared at the ring, I noticed that one of the prongs had stretched, thus releasing the diamond. I was heartsick for many days. On my birthday, my husband, who had searched many jewelers until he found one who could replace the diamond in time for my birthday, returned the ring to me. I cried, jumped up and down, and couldn't stop looking at it. I had never discounted the six diamonds that had always been there, but how I had longed for the lost one. The ring just wasn't complete without it.

We have to value our kids the same way; each one is more precious than any diamond. If they are lost, we need to search and search for them until we find them. We may need help from others to restore them, but we must do this by any means necessary.

To nurture someone is to spend time with the person and care for him or her. We have to give our kids nurturing—when they are eight, twelve, sixteen, twenty-one, or even older. I'm fifty, and I still long to hear my mother's voice and to spend time with her. I will admit, even as a grown person, I get a bit angry when others come over and I have to share her. I do pray and get over it, but I still long to spend time with her all by myself. I believe we all need that at times, perhaps more often than we realize. Some parents may say, "I didn't get that when I was young, so my children will be fine without it." But we are all different individuals, and what if they won't be fine?

When they had finished eating, Jesus said to Simon Peter, "Simon son of John, do you truly love me more than these?" "Yes, Lord," he said, "you know that I love you." Jesus said, "Feed my lambs." Again Jesus said, "Simon son of John, do you truly love me?" He answered, "Yes, Lord, you know that I love you." Jesus said, "Take care of my sheep." The third time he said to him, "Simon son of John, do you love me?" Peter was hurt because Jesus asked him the third time, "Do you love me?" He said, "Lord, you know all things; you know that I love you." Jesus said, "Feed my sheep.

John 21:15-17

When we love and take care of the ones that God has blessed us with, we show that we love God. He said that is how we show our love for Him. Sometimes we take care of everybody except those in our own household. Our children notice how we treat everybody at church so graciously, and this grieves them because it proves we are capable of showing love and spending time with others—we just don't do it with them. I've heard of this happening so many times, and sadly, I myself have sometimes been guilty of this in the past.

When God showed me what I was doing, I didn't like what I saw. I ached for my children. I then decided to watch movies with them, take them to playgrounds and amusement parks, play board games at home, and do many other things with them. I made them first in my life, and my husband and I have never regretted that decision. In fact, a couple of our kids saw us so much at their schools and on field trips that they began rolling their eyes when they saw us coming! That didn't stop us, however, and when they were older, they thanked us for being there.

Timothy, guard what has been entrusted to your care. Turn away from godless chatter and the opposing ideas of what is falsely called knowledge, which some have professed and in so doing have wandered from the faith.

1 Timothy 6:20&21

This Scripture is telling all of us to guard and care for the things God has entrusted to us. As parents, we have been entrusted with our kids, though only for a season. Because I was told that there was a 98 to 99 percent chance that I would never have kids, I have always valued my time with my children. But in our society, we hear so many negative words about children interfering with our lives: "I want to live my life while I am still young." "I want to spend time with just my friends." These may be legitimate issues, but they should never be fulfilled at the expense of our children. It is never appropriate to bring our children along to do everything that we do; they are only children. Sacrifices have to be made for them.

Some people argue it is quality, not quantity, time that counts, but I beg to differ. Children need both quality and quantity. The investment of time we give them now will pay off in their future and ours. They will become self-sufficient, self-reliant, self-confident, self-controlled, and more selfless with others. However, when we listen to the ungodly and selfish advice of others, we wander from our faith in God. We are not trusting in Him to secure all things for our future if we feel as though we are missing out because of all the time we spend with our children.

My husband said one of the reasons he chose me for his wife was that I was a good mother to my son. No, I was not perfect, but he could see that I cared for my child. If a man or woman wants to take over your life and leave out your children, then that person is not for you. If you can't tell the other person that you have a child or children, then that is not a good situation for anyone.

Hear, O Israel: The LORD our God, the LORD is one. Love the LORD your God with all your heart and with all your soul and with all your strength. These commandments that I give you today are to be upon your hearts. Impress them on your children. Talk about them when you sit at home and when you walk along the road, when you lie down and when you get up. Tie them as symbols on your hands and bind them on your foreheads. Write them on the doorframes of your houses and on your gates.

Deuteronomy 6:4-9

In order for us to impress the Word of God on our children, we must be there to teach them and show them the way. We must help them in the things they do and think. The Scripture talks about walking with them, being with them both at night and in the morning. In our homes, God should be honored in the decency of our artwork and our entertainment choices on TV, radio, and the computer. We can monitor these things, however, only if we are physically present. We can watch over our treasures, our children, only if we are there.

Judas and Silas, who themselves were prophets, said much to encourage and strengthen the brothers. After spending some time there, they were sent off by the brothers with the blessing of peace to return to those who had sent them.

Acts 15:32 & 33

Judas and Silas encouraged and strengthened others by spending time with them. Be devoted to one another in brotherly love. Honor one another above yourselves.

Romans 12:10

To be devoted is to be loving, loyal, and faithful. It means to give up oneself or time or energy to some purpose, activity, or person. If we are to be devoted to our brothers in Christ, how much more should we be devoted to our children?

I remember my mother spending a lot of time with her eight kids. We played games like softball, dodge ball, hide-and-seek, red light, rock teacher and others. She took us to the circus, to movies, and to the park for fun and picnics. We often went to the library and participated in trips with the church. I was one of the younger four children in my family, so my perception of our childhood may be different from some of my siblings.

SELF-CONTROL

My son, if you accept my words and store up my commands within you, turning your ear to wisdom and applying your heart to understanding, and if you call out for insight and cry aloud for understanding, and if you look for it as for silver and search for it as for hidden treasure, then you will understand the fear of the LORD and find the knowledge of God. For the LORD gives wisdom, and from his mouth come knowledge and understanding.

Proverbs 2:1-6

This is a recipe for controlling self; on our own, none of us have the ability to be self-controlled. The Word of God in us—reading it, memorizing it, and applying it in our lives—and the help of the Holy Spirit are necessary to control our fleshly selves. This process does not come easy; it requires constantly searching the truths of God. But when we look to Him, He will answer and help us. His answers may not always line up with our expected answers, but Father knows best. That is where faith and trust come into play.

You must teach what is in accord with sound doctrine. Teach the older men to be temperate, worthy of respect, self-controlled, and sound in faith, in love and in endurance. Likewise, teach the older women to be reverent in the way they live, not to be slanderers or addicted to much wine, but to teach what is good. Then they can train the younger women to love their husbands and children,

Titus 2:1-4

But the fruit of the Spirit is love, joy, peace, patience, kindness, goodness, faithfulness, gentleness and self-control.

Galatians 5:22-23

Even though self-control is listed last, it is by no means the least important. It seems to me that it takes all the other fruits to finally gain self-control.

For this very reason, make every effort to add to your faith goodness; and to goodness, knowledge; and to knowledge, self-control; and to self-control, perseverance; and to perseverance, godliness; and to godliness, brotherly kindness; and to brotherly kindness, love.

2 Peter 1:5-7

Knowledge comes before self-control. It takes the knowledge, understanding, and application of God's Word to have true control of self. With it, we can then persevere under sinful attacks and will grow in godliness and love for God. In turn, we will be kind to our brothers with genuine love. Self-control is definitely important for spiritual growth. This is why parents must help their children to learn the Word of God and His ways. It will profit them like nothing else.

You are all sons of the light and sons of the day. We do not belong to the night or to the darkness. So then, let us not be like others, who are asleep, but let us be alert and self-controlled. For those who sleep, sleeps at night, and those who get drunk, get drunk at night. But since we belong to the day, let us be self-controlled, putting on faith and love as a breastplate, and the hope of salvation as a helmet. For God did not appoint us to suffer wrath but to receive salvation through our Lord Jesus Christ. He died for us so that, whether we are awake or asleep, we may live together with him. Therefore encourage one another and build each other up, just as in fact you are doing.

1 Thessalonians 5-5-11

We are not asleep or without knowledge concerning the things of God. Since we are not asleep, then we are not in darkness to the light and truth of God. We are sober and possess the ability to think clearly. It is so important to study God's Word and apply it. Like a lifeboat, it is useless to us unless we read the instructions and apply them.

Therefore, prepare your minds for action; be self-controlled; set your hope fully on the grace to be given you when Jesus Christ is revealed. As obedient children, do not conform to the evil desires you had when you lived in ignorance. But just as he who called you is holy, so be holy in all you do; for it is written: "Be holy, because I am holy."

1 Peter 1:13-16

So that we won't be ignorant, it is important to understand the knowledge of God and obey it. As we get to know God better, we will learn that He wants us to be like Him with the help of the Holy Spirit.

Humble yourselves, therefore, under God's mighty hand, that he may lift you up in due time. Cast all your anxiety on him because he cares for you. Be self-controlled and alert. Your enemy the devil prowls around like a roaring lion looking for someone to devour. Resist him, standing firm in the faith,

1 Peter 5:6-9

Getting one's self under control requires humility. It is a process, and God will take us through it, but the length of time required will depend on us. We have to recognize things that are wrong or simply not good for us and resist those things. When we do just anything we like, we may have to reap the consequences that go with our actions. The enemy loves to make sure that we reap those consequences. The natural flesh can destroy us if we give in to everything it wants.

If we lack self-control, then disorder reigns and we are susceptible to any negative action. Self, however, is not to be served first; on the contrary, Jesus is to be served first. The order of things is God's way first. If we seek Him first, then all other things will be taken care of.

What good is it for a man to gain the whole world, and yet lose or forfeit his very self?

Luke 9:25

We can certainly choose to be selfish and fail to exert self-control; we may even succeed in obtaining many of our self-seeking desires. But those desires and things will pull us down and away from our Father. That is the most terrible loss there could be.

For we know that our old self was crucified with him so that the body of sin might be done away with, that we should no longer be slaves to sin because anyone who has died has been freed from sin.

Romans 6:6-7

If we are not interested in killing the selfish nature, then we will continue to feed it and it will live. But the more we resist the desires of self, the more we kill self-centeredness. We can do this with God's help, which He provided so long ago on the cross. It cannot be accomplished without His help. There is a saying that claims "God helps those who help themselves," but that is neither true nor scriptural. God helps those who finally admit that they can't do it without His help. We are incapable of winning this battle alone.

He said: "Listen, King Jehoshaphat and all who live in Judah and Jerusalem! This is what the LORD says to you: 'Do not be afraid or discouraged because of this vast army. For the battle is not yours, but God's.

2 Chronicles 20:15

You were taught, with regard to your former way of life, to put off your old self, which is being corrupted by its deceitful desires; to be made new in the attitude of your minds; and to put on the new self, created to be like God in true righteousness and holiness.

Ephesians 4:22-24

Lack of self-control corrupts, but newness of mind enables the new self to become transformed into the likeness of God. We do much damage to ourselves when we give in and do whatever we feel like doing. Self-control is best learned and practiced in the younger years. If children are taught self-control in their younger years, they will have an easier time as they grow older.

Since, then, you have been raised with Christ, set your hearts on things above, where Christ is seated at the right hand of God. Set your minds on things above, not on earthly things. For you died, and your life is now hidden with Christ in God. When Christ, who is your[A] *life, appears, then you also will appear with him in glory. Put to death, therefore, whatever belongs to your earthly nature: sexual immorality, impurity, lust, evil desires and greed, which is idolatry. Because of these, the wrath of God is coming. You used to walk in these ways, in the life you once lived. But now you must rid yourselves of all such things as these: anger, rage, malice, slander, and filthy language from your lips. Do not lie to each other, since you have taken off your old self with its practices and have put on the new self, which is being renewed in knowledge in the image of its Creator.*

Colossians 3:1-10

When our minds constantly dwell on the wrong things, and we go over and over all the bad things done to us or the bad things that we want to do to others, then it is already our reality, to a certain degree. We will most likely give in to persuasive actions tempting us if we have already rehearsed them in our minds. If it is necessary to think only on the things of Christ, then we must use whatever means necessary to be successful in this. We must put to death the things in our lives that pertain to sexual immorality (adultery, same-sex sexual relationships, inappropriate behavior with children, sex before marriage, thoughts of being with someone in a sexual manner, etc.), impurity (indecency, lewdness, defilement, pollution), lust (physical appetite, passion for someone or something), evil desires (motives, will, urges), and greed (excessive desire for getting or having, desire for more than one needs or deserves).

Lack of self-control shows itself through anger (a feeling of displeasure resulting from mistreatment), rage (furious and uncontrolled anger, violent anger in action and speech), malice (evil intent, a deliberate and intentional plan to do something wrong), slander (the utterance of a false statement to a second party regarding a third party to damage the person's reputation or character), filthy language (morally vicious and corrupt, disgustingly foul and obscene, profanity), and lying (false, untruthful, dishonest words or actions). For our minds and bodies to be under the control of God, then, reading, studying, and applying the Word is a continuous process. Our minds have to constantly and continuously be renewed. For as long as we live, the process is ongoing.

I admit I am still working on this. My mouth gets me in so much trouble at times. I can't seem to, 100 percent, allow someone else to have the last word. Other times I don't actually say anything, but I give people the silent treatment. I back away from them for a time until I get over whatever they have done to me. This is not right! The Bible says, as far as it lies within me, I am to live at peace with all men. That means I should take the first step to let the offense go.

Make a Stand, Take a Stand

King Asa also deposed his grandmother Maacah from her position as queen mother, because she had made a repulsive Asherah pole. Asa cut the pole down, broke it up and burned it in the Kidron Valley.

2 Chronicles 15:16

Sometimes we may be forced to make a stand against our parents for the sake of what's right. This is never easy, and we will probably be ostracized for it. Nevertheless, we must make a stand for the Lord. We must love what He loves and hate what He hates. If we sometimes have to make a stand against family, then we will certainly have to do it with others too. But we should always do so with kindness and compassion.

No one will be able to stand up against you all the days of your life. As I was with Moses, so I will be with you; I will never leave you nor forsake you.

Joshua 1:5

When we make a stand for what is right, God is on our side. He will not leave us. He's not saying that we won't be persecuted or ever get into trouble, but He does say He will be right there with us.

The LORD said to Joshua, "Stand up! What are you doing down on your face? Israel has sinned; they have violated my covenant, which I commanded them to keep. They have taken some of the devoted things; they have stolen, they have lied, they have put them with their own possessions. That is why the Israelites cannot stand against their enemies; they turn their backs and run because they have been made liable to destruction. I will not be with you anymore unless you destroy whatever among you is devoted to destruction.

Joshua 7:10-12

God told Joshua to make a stand and rebuke the Israelites for their wrongdoing. They needed to be rebuked because they were about to lose God's blessings without even realizing why. God said He would not be with them unless they corrected what they were doing wrong.

The arrogant cannot stand in your presence; you hate all who do wrong.

Psalms 5:5

We have to assume a certain posture in order to make an effective stand. We can't be arrogant and expect people to pay attention to us. In making a stand, we want to persuade people to listen to us so that they will change their behavior or at least consider what is being said. We have to be people of character. God hates all wrongdoing, and we should not only hate sin but also make a stand when necessary, and always in love. The way that we approach people will make a world of difference.

Blessed is the man who does not walk in the counsel of the wicked or stand in the way of sinners or sit in the seat of mockers. But his delight is in the law of the LORD, and on his law he meditates day and night. He is like a tree planted by streams of water, which yields its fruit in season and whose leaf does not wither. Whatever he does prospers.

Psalms 1: 1-4

We are blessed when we do not stand with people who do wrong and could possibly cause us to do wrong. How can we meditate on God and the things of God if we are hanging around those who are trying to persuade us to do things contrary to His way? We must be careful of our acquaintances because those who are close to us get our time and our attention. Some of us are weaker than others. Some of us would rather go with the flow than let others know there is a different way of doing things. But when planted in God, we can be strong and unmovable, like a tree planted near the water, and draw our strength from Jesus, the living water.

If you, O LORD, kept a record of sins, O Lord, who could stand? But with you there is forgiveness; therefore you are feared.

Psalms 130:3 -4

None of us are perfect! We can't look down on other people because of their views. They may not listen to us, but we can pray for them. God does not keep record of our wrongdoing when we ask for forgiveness, and neither should we keep throwing things up to others if they have asked for forgiveness.

We should be patient with others. As adults, we teach this by example to our children and other young people. Unfortunately, many are not doing this. For example, there is so much disrespect shown to our president, both for his position and for the man himself. Although senators and representatives are supposed to be leaders, some of them raise the biggest stink about abortion, spending, or other issues while swallowing the camel whole. They seem to know nothing about love and respect for others and those in authority.

When we make a stand, it should line up with the Word of God—not the word of someone else. Just because someone is a senator, congressional representative, governor, preacher, doctor, lawyer, teacher, or anything else does not mean that what he or she says is 100 percent truth. It may be 90 percent truth with the other 10 percent twisted or omitted, which makes it not the whole truth.

Obey the king's command, I say, because you took an oath before God. Do not be in a hurry to leave the king's presence. Do not stand up for a bad cause, for he will do whatever he pleases. Since a king's word is supreme, who can say to him, "What are you doing?" Whoever obeys his command will come to no harm, and the wise heart will know the proper time and procedure. For there is a proper time and procedure for every matter, though a man's misery weighs heavily upon him.

Ecclesiastes 8:2-6

Finally, be strong in the Lord and in his mighty power. Put on the full armor of God so that you can take your stand against the devil's schemes. For our struggle is not against flesh and blood, but against the rulers, against the authorities, against the powers of this dark world and against the spiritual forces of evil in the heavenly realms. Therefore put on the full armor of God, so that when the day of evil comes, you may be able to stand your ground, and after you have done everything, to stand. Stand firm then, with the belt of truth buckled around your waist, with the breastplate of righteousness in place, and with your feet fitted with the readiness that comes from the gospel of peace. In addition to all this, take up the shield of faith, with which you can extinguish all the flaming arrows of the evil one. Take the helmet of salvation and the sword of the Spirit, which is the word of God. And pray in the Spirit on all occasions with all kinds of prayers and requests. With this in mind, be alert and always keep on praying for all the saints.

Ephesians 6-10-18

Lies and Truth

Jesus consistently said, "I tell you the truth" as He was speaking. In the book of Matthew alone, He made that statement approximately thirty times. Perhaps He said those words primarily for emphasis, because everything He said was obviously true. Possibly, knowing what people were thinking, He knew they did not believe the incredible thing He was saying, or perhaps He knew that the message He spoke was hard to believe. Whatever the reason, Jesus believed in telling the truth.

If any part of a story in not true, then it is not a true story. Truth is a whole unit. We can't call it the whole truth if it is 99.9 percent true, but the remaining small portion untrue. Unlike Ivory soap, the truth must be 100 percent true. Another trend calls lies by pleasant and sweet names, such as white lies, fudging, little lies, gray areas, harmless lies, tweaking the story, and other such phrases.

You used to walk in these ways, in the life you once lived. But now you must rid yourselves of all such things as these: anger, rage, malice, slander, and filthy lan-

guage from your lips. Do not lie to each other, since you have taken off your old self with its sinful ways. And have put on the new self, which is being renewed in knowledge in the image of its Creator.

Colossian 3:7-10

Lying is a part of the self that has not been made new in Christ. After we invite Christ into our hearts, lying should no longer be a steady fixture in our lives. As a matter of fact, it should become less and less common as we are renewed day by day. Paul tells us not to lie, and this is listed after admonitions against anger, rage, malice, slander, and filthy language. Most of these issues concern our treatment of others in some way and separate people in relationships.

Trust cannot be maintained if lying is involved. There is a saying "no man is an island." True, we should not be alone, but no one wants to be in a relationship with someone who can't be trusted. Lying is not a single-package deal. If lying is present, many other evil works are at the party also. It never travels alone! Its entourage always hangs around to join in the fun.

Then Peter said, "Ananias, how is it that Satan has so filled your heart that you have lied to the Holy Spirit and have kept for yourself some of the money you received for the land? Didn't it belong to you before it was sold? And after it was sold, wasn't the money at your disposal? What made you think of doing such a thing? You have not lied to men but to God."

Acts 5:3-4

When we decide to lie, we are not just committing an offense against a person, but against God Himself. The Holy Spirit that dwells in us takes offense when we lie to or about someone. False statements offend Him just as much as do gossip or physical harm directed toward others. For example, we should never make idle boasts about what we will give or have given to the church. It is not people we should desire to impress.

Ultimately, when we lie to others, we lie to God. Whatever we do to the least of people, we do it to Him. He takes all behavior so personally. As a mother, I take things personally that involve my children. I will go out of my way to repay and aid someone who has done something nice for my children. On the other hand, it hurts me personally if someone does something bad to one of my children. It is as though that act has been done to me. In the same way, God is in tune to us and the things that pertain to us.

I call on the LORD in my distress, and he answers me. Save me, O LORD, from lying lips and from deceitful tongues. What will he do to you, and what more besides, O deceitful tongue? He will punish you with a warrior's sharp arrows, with burning coals of the broom tree.

Psalms 120:1-4

We cause distress in others when we lie and are deceitful to them. It seems that we are at war and fighting for our lives. Punishment is severe for liars; sharp arrows and burning coals are their reward. I know for myself that as a child, I was punished for every lie I told. My mother's hand exacted punishment with every word of correction she spoke. She might say, "Didn't I tell you not to lie anymore? I told you to tell the truth, or it would cost you." That is twenty words, and with those twenty words, I had twenty reminders of the consequences lying brought.

There are six things the LORD hates, seven that are detestable to him: haughty eyes, a lying tongue, hands that shed innocent blood, a heart that devises wicked schemes, feet that are quick to rush into evil, a false witness who pours out lies and a man who stirs up dissension among brothers.

Proverbs 6:16-19

Four of the things listed in this passage deal with lying. Since God is truth, the whole truth, and nothing but the truth, He will accept nothing less than the complete and total truth. People who lie cannot be trusted to either receive or give information. They are tainted in all their actions. They view the world in a different way from others. It is as though they place themselves above everyone else to manipulate things according to the way they want situations to end.

Truthful lips endure forever, but a lying tongue lasts only a moment.

Proverbs 12:19

A lying person will not last, but the truth brings a legacy that lives on and on.
A fortune made by a lying tongue is a fleeting vapor and a deadly snare.

Proverbs 21

One lie always leads to another to cover up for the first one, but eventually lies catch up with the ones who spoke them. Although some people obtain certain jobs by lying about their credentials, they will have to back up their words with their actions. Consequently, their jobs may be short lived. Also, riches and wealth gained through lying will be short lived. Lying on a college application for admission will eventually lead to being expelled from school. Lying is a false foundation, and it will always crumble.

A lying tongue hates those it hurts, and a flattering mouth works ruin.

Proverbs 26:28

If we love someone, we will tell that person the truth. It does not benefit friends and relatives to be told lies in order to make them feel better. It is not good to tell others they possess certain talents they clearly don't possess. Why tell people they can sing and dance when clearly they can't? Eventually they will be told the truth by someone who doesn't care about their feelings. Then they will be hurt and want to know why you were not truthful with them in the first place. As I said earlier, singing is not a gift the Lord has given me, but I wasted nearly twenty years of my life in a singing group because no one told me the truth. A lot of time was wasted because I couldn't face the truth myself, and no one told me otherwise.

You have profaned me among my people for a few handfuls of barley and scraps of bread. By lying to my people, who listen to lies, you have killed those who should not have died and have spared those who should not live.

Ezekiel 13:19

Some people will sell others out for little or nothing. They will lie and help people who do not need help, and they will not take up for those who do need help. Under no circumstances should we lie. Lies save the guilty while sweeping the truth under the rug to the detriment of the innocent.

Do not withhold your mercy from me, O LORD; may your love and your truth always protect me.

Psalms 40:11

The truth is a protection. If we always tell the truth, we won't have to try to remember what we said at an earlier time. It may not always seem like it, but the truth needs to be told, even if it causes a problem at the time. God will work all things for our good when we live according to His purpose. He said so in His Word.

I've known many parents who have turned their kids in to the law, realizing that if they let them go unpunished for unlawful deeds, they will never learn the consequences of their actions. I have had to do something similar with one of my own children. The behavior was not something illegal, but it was against God's law and the school's policy, so I couldn't allow that child to get away with the behavior. When we cover up for our children, we are teaching them to hide the truth if it serves a purpose at the time, but that is not how God deals with us. God loves us, and even though He forgives our sins, He still requires us to bear responsibility for our actions.

Send forth your light and your truth, let them guide me; let them bring me to your holy mountain, to the place where you dwell. Then will I go to the altar of God, to God, my joy and my delight. I will praise you with the harp, O God, my God.

Psalms 43:3-4

The truth, not our brand or spin on what we call the truth, clears the path for us to stand before God. Lies make us filthy and prevent us from standing before a holy and righteous God. Truth and light stand together, and lies and darkness stand together. Lies and light will never coexist. God is a spirit, and they that worship Him must do so in spirit and in truth.

Against you, you only, have I sinned and done what is evil in your sight, so that you are proved right when you speak and justified when you judge. Surely I was sinful at birth, sinful from the time my mother conceived me. Surely you desire truth in the inner parts; you teach me wisdom in the inmost place.

Psalms 51:4-6

We are also required to be truthful in our inner thoughts. We cannot verbally claim to love someone but hate the individual in our thoughts. This is contradictory, and it is a lie. We are not behaving in a manner consistent with what we think. That is not to say that we shouldn't be nice to people even when we don't feel like it. I think we should do this until it really comes from the heart. What we should avoid is intentional hypocrisy in our actions towards others with no intention to grow in love towards them.

You love evil rather than good, falsehood rather than speaking the truth. Selah You love every harmful word, O you deceitful tongue! Surely God will bring you down to everlasting ruin.

Psalms 52:3-5

In today's society, what is good according to God's standard is looked down upon by a large number of people. It is even sad to say that many Christians think the Bible is too extreme, though our Father knows best. Some people love to tell lies, and they think they are clever if they are very good at it. I was one of those people in my past. But thank God that is now my past! Such people will have their day because God will bring them down. Whatever is done in the dark will be brought to the light. This is a promise from God.

Teach me your way, O LORD, and I will walk in your truth; give me an undivided heart, that I may fear your name. I will praise you, O Lord my God, with all my heart; I will glorify your name forever. For great is your love toward me; you have delivered me from the depths of the grave.

Psalms 86:11-13

In truly knowing the ways of the Lord, we will walk in the way of truth. Lies come from a divided heart, from wanting things or circumstances to be different from what is true. We don't like the way things really are, so with our mouths, we try to create a new, unreal, and untrue way. The reason lies eventually collapse is that they are built on falsehood rather than reality. It takes more lies to hold up the first lie that was created.

God wants to deliver us from the grave of lies that we so often dig for ourselves. He desires truth from us because He loves us and wants what is best and what is real for us. We don't surprise Him by anything we say or do because He knows our thoughts before they become actions. He knows what is in our hearts. This is the reason we should read and study the Bible, because the Holy Spirit in us will rise up against every lie that wants to come forth. However, the fact is, we are given a free will, and we choose what proceeds out of our mouths. The choice is ours to make, and we must set our minds on the truth, regardless of the consequences.

I have chosen the way of truth; I have set my heart on your laws.

Psalms 119:30

Kings take pleasure in honest lips; they value a man who speaks the truth.

Proverbs 16:13

Most people want to be around honest people. Only immature, foolish people want to be around those who lie and tell them only the things they want to hear.

They will eventually come across someone who will tell them the truth and down will come the façade. Most leaders desire truthful people around them. This helps them and keeps them out of trouble. On the other hand, there are some leaders who like to have people around who will lie for them. If the head is corrupt, so are the other parts of the body; however, they will not endure.

For our offenses are many in your sight, and our sins testify against us. Our offenses are ever with us, and we acknowledge our iniquities: rebellion and treachery against the LORD, turning our backs on our God, fomenting oppression and revolt, uttering lies our hearts have conceived. So justice is driven back, and righteousness stands at a distance; truth has stumbled in the streets, honesty cannot enter. Truth is nowhere to be found, and whoever shuns evil becomes a prey.

Isaiah 59:12-15

When we tell a lie, justice and righteousness are driven from the picture. Sadly, lies that masquerade as truth are so often told today that the truth alone is not enough. It has to be embellished to make it more appealing, more interesting, or more entertaining. Honesty does not and cannot enter into such a place. The sad thing is, those who tell the truth are often attacked, but we must accept the consequences and stand up for the truth anyway.

"When you tell them all this, they will not listen to you; when you call to them, they will not answer. Therefore say to them, 'This is the nation that has not obeyed the LORD its God or responded to correction. Truth has perished; it has vanished from their lips. Cut off your hair and throw it away; take up a lament on the barren heights, for the LORD has rejected and abandoned this generation that is under his wrath.

Jeremiah 7:27-29

This nation had not obeyed God, and truth was nowhere to be found. These people didn't know the truth, and therefore they didn't tell the truth. Though God is truth, they didn't recognize Him. Apparently, they had known Him at one time, but now they didn't even respond when He tried to correct them to bring them back to Himself. God was trying to show mercy, but they never ceased their sinning and continued to defy Him.

"They make ready their tongue like a bow, to shoot lies; it is not by truth that they triumph in the land. They go from one sin to another; they do not acknowledge me," declares the LORD. "Beware of your friends; do not trust your brothers. For every brother is a deceiver, and every friend a slanderer. Friend deceives friend, and no one speaks the truth. They have taught their tongues to lie; they weary them-

selves with sinning. You live in the midst of deception; in their deceit they refuse to acknowledge me," declares the LORD. Therefore this is what the LORD Almighty says: "See, I will refine and test them, for what else can I do because of the sin of my people? Their tongue is a deadly arrow; it speaks with deceit. With his mouth each speaks cordially to his neighbor, but in his heart he sets a trap for him. Should I not punish them for this?" declares the LORD. "Should I not avenge myself on such a nation as this?"

Jeremiah 9:3-9

God does not like it when we do things for show. He wants our actions to come from the heart. Lying, cheating, and deceiving all start in the mind and heart. If lying is continually part of our lives, then sadly, it becomes natural to us. That means we have not guarded our hearts and minds, for this is where the issues and decisions of life are formed.

A lying tongue is hurtful, just like a deadly arrow. It pierces and damages the souls of others, and it hurts God. Why would He say He would avenge Himself if it did not harm Him and the ones He loves? When we make the decision to live in sin and ignore what we know about living for the Lord, then we are rejecting Him and choosing a way that is not His.

To the pure, all things are pure, but to those who are corrupted and do not believe, nothing is pure. In fact, both their minds and consciences are corrupted. They claim to know God, but by their actions they deny him. They are detestable, disobedient and unfit for doing anything good.

Titus 1:15-16

This is the message we have heard from him and declare to you: God is light; in him there is no darkness at all. If we claim to have fellowship with him yet walk in the darkness, we lie and do not live by the truth. But if we walk in the light, as he is in the light, we have fellowship with one another, and the blood of Jesus, his Son, purifies us from all sin.

1 John 1:5-7

Our choice in the type of life we live shows whether we acknowledge God as Lord. I'm glad the Lord is revealing the things in my life that could be considered lies. For example, if my husband inquires about some money I spent, and I tell him I bought groceries, paid a bill, and gave to the church, but leave out the fact that I spent fifty dollars buying an expensive pair of earrings, and then I have not told the whole truth. If I have done nothing wrong, then why do I hide the earrings? When I wear them later and my husband says he has never seen them before, why do I answer that I've had them for a while or that he just doesn't remember them? All this deception and all these lies are not worth the price of the earrings. Did I need or want them that badly? No, of course not. With all the added deception, they became even more expensive than they were originally. When truth is covered with other statements, it becomes harder to identify. Truth needs nothing attached to it or standing alongside of it. Truth stands alone.

This need for truth also applies to husbands as they relate to their wives. If a wife ask her husband whom he went to lunch with, and he names everyone but a certain person whose motives towards him she distrust, then he has lied. Why is it necessary to omit this person's name? Is this secret more important than his wife's feelings?

One final example: If someone that I don't want to talk to calls my home, and I tell the person who answered the phone, "Wait; let me run outside the door so you can tell the person I'm not home," this, too is a lie.

Our children need to be taught to speak the truth, the whole truth, and nothing but the truth, and we must model it before them.

Good Stewards of Money, Time, and Talents

There are several definitions for *steward*. A steward may be a person who acts as a supervisor or administrator for another person, or a person who is morally responsible for the careful use of money, time, talents, or other resources of a community or particular group. As stewards, we are to care for others with the money, time, and talents that God has blessed us with. An important way to show God we love Him is to love and care for others. He created us all, but He has given more resources to some, and they are to look out for His other children.

'If one of your countrymen becomes poor and is unable to support himself among you, help him as you would an alien or a temporary resident, so he can continue to live among you. Do not take interest of any kind from him, but fear your God, so that your countryman may continue to live among you. You must not lend him money at interest or sell him food at a profit. I am the LORD your God, who brought you out of Egypt to give you the land of Canaan and to be your God.

Leviticus 25:35-38

The Scriptures tell us on numerous occasions to love our neighbor as ourselves, but how do we apply this to our personal lives? Does the Bible mean this literally, or are such statements there just to take up space? I believe the Bible means it literally because this principle is stated so many times.

We are separate from the people who live beside us, but we are also connected. But God's instruction to love our neighbor applies to more than just the people who live near us; God wants us to love and care for many others. Yes, we are supposed to take care of our immediate families and households first, but the reason God blesses us with excess is not so we can hoard it for ourselves, but so we can help others. We are blessed to be a blessing!

We are not to profit at the expense of someone who has lost his income and is struggling to care for his family. On the other hand, we are not to perpetuate laziness in others. Proverbs says if a man doesn't work, he shouldn't eat. If a man is working hard but still can't feed himself or his family, then we should help. If he sits around his home and does not go out and apply for work or even barter services he can provide, should we consistently assist him? Every case should be dealt with individually, and we should pray and ask God for help to discern His will.

Do not charge your brother interest, whether on money or food or anything else that may earn interest. You may charge a foreigner interest, but not a brother Israelite, so that the LORD your God may bless you in everything you put your hand to in the land you are entering to possess. If you make a vow to the LORD your God, do not be slow to pay it, for the LORD your God will certainly demand it of you and you will be guilty of sin. But if you refrain from making a vow, you will not be guilty. Whatever your lips utter you must be sure to do, because you made your vow freely to the LORD your God with your own mouth. If you enter your neighbor's vineyard, you may eat all the grapes you want, but do not put any in your basket. If you enter your neighbor's grainfield, you may pick kernels with your hands, but you must not put a sickle to his standing grain.

Deuteronomy 23:19-25

He said: "Go up to Hilkiah the high priest and have him get ready the money that has been brought into the temple of the LORD, which the doorkeepers have collected from the people. Have them entrust it to the men appointed to supervise the work on the temple. And have these men pay the workers who repair the temple of the LORD— the carpenters, the builders and the masons. Also have them purchase timber and dressed stone to repair the temple. But they need not account for the money entrusted to them, because they are acting faithfully."

2 Kings 22:4-7

In this passage, the people had given money to help with the building of the temple. The money was to be used for that purpose and that purpose alone. The same is true for us in our money management. When we designate money for a specific purpose, then we should use it for that purpose only. All responsibilities should be taken care of before money is spent on other things. Grocery money should be used for groceries, rent or mortgage money should be used for the rent or mortgage, and tithes should be used for the church and God's people.

God blesses people with money to give to the church, but if someone in the church misuses it, the guilt is not on the one who gave. The guilt is on the abuser, and God will take care of that situation. If church leaders have proven themselves faithful, we can trust them to do what is right.

Dishonest money dwindles away, but he who gathers money little by little makes it grow.

Proverbs 13:11

If we attain money in a dishonest way, it will soon be gone. Also, if we are not wise in handling money, it will quickly disappear. When we work hard for what we get, we tend to appreciate it and value it more. We give more thought, then, to how we spend it.

Of what use is money in the hand of a fool, since he has no desire to get wisdom?

Proverbs 17:16

We spoke about this in the previous verse. Money in the hand of a fool is quickly spent. Fools do not act wisely with money because they have not searched for the wisdom needed to make good decisions. They may think they are wise, but their money cannot seem to stay with them. Fools often think themselves wise when in reality they are not.

Whoever loves money never has money enough; whoever loves wealth is never satisfied with his income. This too is meaningless. As goods increase, so do those who consume them. And what benefit are they to the owner except to feast his eyes on them? The sleep of a laborer is sweet, whether he eats little or much, but the abundance of a rich man permits him no sleep. I have seen a grievous evil under the sun: wealth hoarded to the harm of its owner, or wealth lost through some misfortune, so that when he has a son there is nothing left for him. Naked a man comes from his mother's womb, and as he comes, so he departs. That he can carry in his hand.

Ecclesiastes 5:10-15

We cannot allow ourselves to be in love with money and unable to use it when there is a need. God blesses us with money and then allows others in need to cross our paths. We should seek God concerning to whom we should give money or help in some other way.

Those with much money tend to worry about how to keep it safe and how to increase it, but they seldom worry about how to help others with it. Their wealth can actually make them sick from the worrying and sleeplessness that accompany it. The fact is, however, we are only borrowers of any money we have, because we will not carry it with us to the grave.

Wisdom is a shelter as money is a shelter, but the advantage of knowledge is this: that wisdom preserves the life of its possessor.

Ecclesiastes 7:12

Wisdom is needed to accompany wealth. Money can and will be wasted if we are not smart in its use. Wisdom on how to spend money will preserve our lives.

If a man is lazy, the rafters sag; if his hands are idle, the house leaks.

Ecclesiastes 10:18

A lazy man does not even take care of the place where he lives. It is as though he hopes the responsibility will fall on someone else. He does not use whatever money he has to provide for his basic needs.

Cast your bread upon the waters, for after many days you will find it again. Give portions to seven, yes to eight, for you do not know what disaster may come upon the land.

Ecclesiastes 11:1

It is always better to plant seeds of giving in times of plenty. When we do, we are opening the door to receiving God's blessings as well as help from others in our time of need. This, however, should not be the reason for our giving. Love should be the ultimate reason for helping others, and we should help as many people as possible.

"No one can serve two masters. Either he will hate the one and love the other, or he will be devoted to the one and despise the other. You cannot serve both God and money.

Matthew 6:24

Money is good to have, but it must be kept in its proper place. It should not dominate our lives, nor should our quest to get more money take precedence over our relationship with the Father. We will show more allegiance to one or the other, and our spending and time will tell the story of our true priority.

"But he answered one of them, 'Friend, I am not being unfair to you. Didn't you agree to work for a denarius? Take your pay and go. I want to give the man who was hired last the same as I gave you. Don't I have the right to do what I want with my own money? Or are you envious because I am generous?

Matthew 20:13-15

Others will judge the way we spend our money, but we answer only to God for its use, for it is He who is the giver of money. Some will say, "Don't I have the right to spend my money the way that I want?" The answer is no. God has a plan for our lives, and there is a plan for the money He blesses us with.

"Again, it will be like a man going on a journey, who called his servants and entrusted his property to them. To one he gave five talents of money, to another two talents, and to another one talent, each according to his ability. Then he went on his journey. The man who had received the five talents went at once and put his money to work and gained five more. So also, the one with the two talents gained two more. But the man who had received the one talent went off, dug a hole in the ground and hid his master's money. "After a long time the master of those servants returned and settled accounts with them. The man who had received the five talents brought the other five. 'Master,' he said, 'you entrusted me with five talents. See, I have gained five more.' "His master replied, 'Well done, good and faithful servant!

Pass the Blessings!

You have been faithful with a few things; I will put you in charge of many things. Come and share your master's happiness!' "The man with the two talents also came. 'Master,' he said, 'you entrusted me with two talents; see, I have gained two more.' "His master replied, 'Well done, good and faithful servant! You have been faithful with a few things; I will put you in charge of many things. Come and share your master's happiness!' "Then the man who had received the one talent came. 'Master,' he said, 'I knew that you are a hard man, harvesting where you have not sown and gathering where you have not scattered seed. So I was afraid and went out and hid your talent in the ground. See, here is what belongs to you.' "His master replied, 'You wicked, lazy servant! So you knew that I harvest where I have not sown and gather where I have not scattered seed? Well then, you should have put my money on deposit with the bankers, so that when I returned I would have received it back with interest. "'Take the talent from him and give it to the one who has the ten talents. For everyone who has will be given more, and he will have an abundance. Whoever does not have, even what he has will be taken from him. And throw that worthless servant outside, into the darkness, where there will be weeping and gnashing of teeth.'

Matthew 25:14-30

This Scripture passage says many different things to many different people, but it tells me not to squander the blessings of God. Even if I have only one talent, I am not excused from using that one. I should invest that one talent into others, and God will multiply it.

I feel like I can do many things, but I don't know whether I should do all those things or if enough time remains in my life to accomplish all the things that I want to do. I do know that I am listening to the Father, and when He says "go" on a particular thing, then I will go. Also, if I am doing something I feel the Father wants me to do, and He says "enough" at any point, then that is enough. The thing that is good at this moment may not be good for the next moment. I might be allowed to do that thing just long enough to be a blessing to one specific person, but when that time is over, then it is over. The same may also be true about people in our lives. Some people may be in our lives for a certain period time just to be a blessing to us. God cares about each one of us just that much.

"Whoever can be trusted with very little can also be trusted with much, and whoever is dishonest with very little will also be dishonest with much. So if you have not been trustworthy in handling worldly wealth, who will trust you with true riches? And if you have not been trustworthy with someone else's property, who will give you property of your own? "No servant can serve two masters. Either he will hate the one and love the other, or he will be devoted to the one and despise the other. You cannot serve both God and money." The Pharisees, who loved money, heard all this and were sneering at Jesus. He said to them, "You are the ones who justify

yourselves in the eyes of men, but God knows your hearts. What is highly valued among men is detestable in God's sight.

Luke 16:10-15

As stewards, we determine the amount of money that God can truly bless us with. It is sad when a person not skilled in handling finances receives a large sum of money. Of course, *large* is relative to the person's perspective. While one thousand dollars is a lot of money to one person, another person considers a million dollars to be a lot, and yet another, a hundred million dollars. Whatever the case, money can leave a person quickly if he or she lacks wisdom. Large sums of money can become a master to people because now they have to protect it and keep others from taking it. Also, there is the temptation of spending it quickly on fleshly desires. For some people, money separates them from God, who is the giver of the gift.

While they were listening to this, he went on to tell them a parable, because he was near Jerusalem and the people thought that the kingdom of God was going to appear at once. He said: "A man of noble birth went to a distant country to have himself appointed king and then to return. So he called ten of his servants and gave them ten minas. 'Put this money to work,' he said, 'until I come back.' "But his subjects hated him and sent a delegation after him to say, 'We don't want this man to be our king.' "He was made king, however, and returned home. Then he sent for the servants to whom he had given the money, in order to find out what they had gained with it. "The first one came and said, 'Sir, your mina has earned ten more.'" 'Well done, my good servant!' his master replied. 'Because you have been trustworthy in a very small matter, take charge of ten cities.' "The second came and said, 'Sir, your mina has earned five more.' "His master answered, 'You take charge of five cities.' "Then another servant came and said, 'Sir, here is your mina; I have kept it laid away in a piece of cloth. I was afraid of you, because you are a hard man. You take out what you did not put in and reap what you did not sow.' "His master replied, 'I will judge you by your own words, you wicked servant! You knew, did you, that I am a hard man, taking out what I did not put in, and reaping what I did not sow? Why then didn't you put my money on deposit, so that when I came back, I could have collected it with interest?' "Then he said to those standing by, 'Take his mina away from him and give it to the one who has ten minas.'

Luke 19:11-24

I believe the key here is that the first two men put the money to work until their master returned. We should not just bury money to keep it safe, because then it cannot grow. We should work to increase the money of others that is in our possession. However, some people feel that if something does not belong to them, then they do not have to care for it as carefully. Rental cars, hotel accommodations, rented videos, and other such items are not treated carefully because these things do not belong to them. But if we can't take care of material possessions in our care temporarily, how can we be trusted with things for ourselves? It shows responsibility and consideration to be a steward of others' possessions. We should be in charge of money instead of it being in charge of us.

But one of his disciples, Judas Iscariot, who was later to betray him, objected, 5"Why wasn't this perfume sold and the money given to the poor? It was worth a year's wages." 6He did not say this because he cared about the poor but because he was a thief; as keeper of the money bag, he used to help himself to what was put into it. 7"Leave her alone," Jesus replied. "It was intended that she should save this perfume for the day of my burial. 8You will always have the poor among you, but you will not always have me."

John 12:4-8

Woe to us if we are in charge of money for an organization and misuse the funds! Such people misuse money so that there will be more for them to steal for themselves. In the Scripture, we can see what happened to Judas. Greed overtook and blinded him. He had direct access to Jesus, the Son of God, yet the love of money blinded him. He was so busy stealing and isolating himself from the fellowship and miracles around him that he missed heaven and all its glory. He died a horrible death. When we are in charge of someone else's money, we should carefully follow the plan that has been established.

When he saw Peter and John about to enter, he asked them for money. Peter looked straight at him, as did John. Then Peter said, "Look at us!" So the man gave them his attention, expecting to get something from them. Then Peter said, "Silver or gold I do not have, but what I have I give you. In the name of Jesus Christ of Nazareth, walk." Taking him by the right hand, he helped him up, and instantly the man's feet and ankles became strong. He jumped to his feet and began to walk. Then he went with them into the temple courts, walking and jumping, and praising God.

Acts 3:3-8

This is a case of being a good steward of our talents and spiritual gifts. We may not have money to share with others, but we will always have Jesus to share, and He is more than enough. Yes, we should take care of physical needs if we are able to do so, but it is just as important to share our spiritual gifts. Freely we have received; we should be generous in our giving.

There were no needy persons among them. For from time to time those who owned lands or houses sold them, brought the money from the sales and put it at the apostles' feet, and it was distributed to anyone as he had need.

Acts 4:34-35

I don't think that God requires all of us to go this far, but He does ask some to give at higher levels than others. These people know who they are, and they can and do learn to be givers at this level. However, we can all help others in many ways, whether financially, spiritually, physically, or socially. The object is to give if we can spare it without forsaking our own responsibilities. In the following Scriptures, we learn to take care of our responsibilities first. We can't give if we don't have it to spare.

"At that time the kingdom of heaven will be like ten virgins who took their lamps and went out to meet the bridegroom. Five of them were foolish and five were wise. The foolish ones took their lamps but did not take any oil with them. The wise, however, took oil in jars along with their lamps. The bridegroom was a long time in coming, and they all became drowsy and fell asleep. "At midnight the cry rang out: 'Here's the bridegroom! Come out to meet him!' "Then all the virgins woke up and trimmed their lamps. The foolish ones said to the wise, 'Give us some of your oil; our lamps are going out.' "'No,' they replied, 'there may not be enough for both us

and you. Instead, go to those who sell oil and buy some for yourselves.' "But while they were on their way to buy the oil, the bridegroom arrived. The virgins who were ready went in with him to the wedding banquet. And the door was shut. "Later the others also came. 'Sir! Sir!' they said. 'Open the door for us!' "But he replied, 'I tell you the truth, I don't know you.' "Therefore keep watch, because you do not know the day or the hour.

Matthew 25:1-13

If the virgins with the extra oil had given it away, they would not have had enough at the time when they needed it. They would have missed out because of giving what they didn't have to spare. Unless we feel the Lord specifically and definitely directing us to give away money earmarked for bills, we should not do this. The Bible says to owe no man, and if we have bills, we owe the money to the creditors. My understanding is that we should love and help others in place of purchasing extra houses, cars, boats, clothes, shoes, or entertainment. I'm not saying anything is wrong with these things, but I am saying how can we do this if a brother or sister is hungry? If we all gave unselfishly, I don't think there would be hungry people in the world.

Now about the collection for God's people: Do what I told the Galatians churches to do. On the first day of every week, each one of you should set aside a sum of money in keeping with his income, saving it up, so that when I come no collections will have to be made.

1 Corinthians 16:1-2

If we all gave our tithes and offerings, churches could take care of many needs. Also, if a large portion of the money given to churches wasn't wasted on extravagant buildings and expensive clothes, cars, and other extras for the church staff, many needs could be taken care of. It is not God's desire for there to be so much waste in the world. He has blessed many of us with more than we need, and we are to share it with others.

But godliness with contentment is great gain. For we brought nothing into the world, and we can take nothing out of it. But if we have food and clothing, we will be content with that. People who want to get rich fall into temptation and a trap and into many foolish and harmful desires that plunge men into ruin and destruction. For the love of money is a root of all kinds of evil. Some people, eager for money, have wandered from the faith and pierced themselves with many griefs.

1 Timothy 6:6-10

Are we content with little, or does it require much for us to be content, or are we never contented regardless of how much money we have? No matter which category we fall into, it is certain we will take nothing with us when we leave this world. Certain behaviors and adjustments go along with the territory of having riches. When we have much in our possession, then we have to work to take care of it and keep it safe. The selfishness that comes along with having much money can drive some people to act differently from their usual selves. The determination to keep and increase their money will drive some to harm and destruction. Unfortunately, many people have abandoned their faith and trust in God because of their love, desire, and protection of money. But the good news is, He gave, He gives, and He will give. It's all His!

Keep your lives free from the love of money and be content with what you have, because God has said, "Never will I leave you; never will I forsake you." So we say with confidence, "The Lord is my helper; I will not be afraid. What can man do to me?"

*Hebrews 13:5-***6**

The problem is, we want more, more, and more money, but we want to keep it for ourselves. We can be confident in the fact that God will help us, regardless of our financial status. He won't leave us, and He won't forsake us. Whatever we go through, He will walk with us and make all things better.

Pass the Blessings!

Now listen, you who say, "Today or tomorrow we will go to this or that city, spend a year there, carry on business and make money." Why, you do not even know what will happen tomorrow. What is your life? You are a mist that appears for a little while and then vanishes. Instead, you ought to say, "If it is the Lord's will, we will live and do this or that." As it is, you boast and brag. All such boasting is evil. Anyone, then, who knows the good he ought to do and doesn't do it, sins.

James 4:13-17

We are so presumptuous with our plans, when in reality we don't know if we will be alive in the next moment. Our plans should include God because He alone knows if we will be around tomorrow. It is sinful if we don't do the good we could do when we know we should do it. We can deceive ourselves and others and act as though we didn't know we should have given or helped someone, but God knows our hearts and every thought. Simply put, it is sinful to ignore the genuine needs of our neighbors. "Love your neighbor" is the summation of both the law and the prophets.

Failure to Plan Is a Plan to Fail

For I know the plans I have for you," declares the LORD, "plans to prosper you and not to harm you, plans to give you hope and a future. Then you will call upon me and come and pray to me, and I will listen to you. You will seek me and find me when you seek me with all your heart. I will be found by you," declares the Lord.

Jeremiah 29:11-14

God has a plan for each of us, and it does not change. It is His desire for us to know that plan, and if we seek Him, we will find Him. Keep in mind, His plans may not match the plans we have for ourselves or our children.

"'But if you do not drive out the inhabitants of the land, those you allow to remain will become barbs in your eyes and thorns in your sides. They will give you trouble in the land where you will live. And then I will do to you what I plan to do to them.'

Numbers 33:55-56

This Scripture reminds me of the relationships in our lives. The people that we hang around will either be good for us or they will be trouble for us. Their problems will be our problems. We must, therefore, make conscious decisions regarding the people in our lives. This is sometimes particularly difficult for young people because of the acceptance issues that concern them.

In any relationship, we should ask ourselves, how will this person and I help each other to grow and be better? If the other person does not benefit us in a positive way, then we need to rethink the relationship and its future. This applies to nearly all our relationships, including relationships that may lead to marriage and relationships with business partners. This may also apply to jobs that we accept. Although we cannot choose our relatives, they do not have to be a part of our lives if they hurt us, speak negatively towards us, or constantly bring us down.

Some worthless scoundrels gathered around him and opposed Rehoboam son of Solomon when he was young and indecisive and not strong enough to resist them.

2 Chronicle 13:7

I really wish kids would listen to their parents when they give them advice about some of their friends. Sometimes other people can see things that we can't. We must decide what we want to accomplish in life and then choose people who also want to be successful. Choosing ungodly people as our close friends and advisors can be detrimental if we are not strong enough to discern between true wisdom and foolish talk from lack of knowledge.

They encourage each other in evil plans, they talk about hiding their snares; they say, "Who will see them?" 6They plot injustice and say, "We have devised a perfect plan!" Surely the mind and heart of man are cunning.

Psalms 64:5-6

It amazes me when we think that we can hide things from God. He knows the intents of our hearts.

Nothing in all creation is hidden from God's sight. Everything is uncovered and laid bare before the eyes of him to whom we must give account.

Hebrews 4:13

When we make plans to hurt others, God sees it all. He desires for us to make better decisions, but we have free will, and the choice is up to us. If we hang around people with bad intentions, what will become of us? We will slowly become numb and passive and overlook the things they do. By choosing friends who inspire us to do better, our future plans will flow with greater ease.

Keep me, O LORD, from the hands of the wicked; protect me from men of violence who plan to trip my feet. Proud men have hidden a snare for me; they have spread out the cords of their net and have set traps for me along my path. Selah O LORD, I say to you, "You are my God." Hear, O LORD, my cry for mercy. O Sovereign LORD, my strong deliverer, who shields my head in the day of battle— do not grant the wicked their desires, O LORD; do not let their plans succeed, or they will become proud.

Psalms 140:4-8

As we plan for a successful future, we must be aware that bad people will purposefully set traps for us. They may give us bad advice that they know will make us fall. Not only do perceived friends sometimes cause us to fall, but also coworkers sometimes cause it. Some people will step all over others to advance themselves. We cannot share our plans and goals for the future with everyone. Sometimes it is best if some things are kept between us and the Lord.

Do not those who plot evil go astray? But those who plan what is good find love and faithfulness. All hard work brings a profit, but mere talk leads only to poverty.

Proverbs 14:22-23

If we want to succeed, it will require planning, hard work, and prayer. Our plans must not involve hurting someone else or pulling others down in our efforts to advance. In making good plans for ourselves and others, we will reap love and faithfulness.

Blessed is the man who does not walk in the counsel of the wicked or stand in the way of sinners or sit in the seat of mockers. But his delight is in the law of the LORD, and on his law he meditates day and night. He is like a tree planted by streams of water, which yields its fruit in season and whose leaf does not wither. Whatever he does prospers.

Psalms 1:1-3

If we do not act on the advice of the wicked or keep company with them, but rather we seek God for guidance, the outcome of our plans will be great. We will be like trees continuously watered, and we will bear the wonderful fruit that such trees yield. We will go forth and succeed. This does not mean that God's answers will always be yes, nor does it mean we will never go through hard times. It does mean, however, that we will never walk alone. God will work all things out for our good if we are following His call for our lives.

"All this," David said, "I have in writing from the hand of the LORD upon me, and he gave me understanding in all the details of the plan." David also said to Solomon his son, "Be strong and courageous, and do the work. Do not be afraid

Pass the Blessings!

or discouraged, for the LORD God, my God, is with you. He will not fail you or forsake you until all the work for the service of the temple of the LORD is finished. The divisions of the priests and Levites are ready for all the work on the temple of God, and every willing man skilled in any craft will help you in all the work.

1 Chronicle 28:19-21

We do not have to struggle alone with God's plans for us. He has set others into position to help. I firmly believe the following Scripture that says: And we know that in all things God works for the good of those who love him, who have been called according to his purpose.

Romans 8:28

When we are following God's purpose, then He will make all things work for our good. Even the bad things will be stepping stones to better things to come. We cannot overlook the part in this Scripture that promises this for those who love God. If we love Him, we will keep His commandments. In following God, we can't go wrong.

A wicked man puts up a bold front, but an upright man gives thought to his ways. There is no wisdom, no insight, no plan that can succeed against the LORD. The horse is made ready for the day of battle, but victory rests with the LORD.

Proverbs 21:29-31

It is good to give thought to the things we are considering doing. If we make plans contrary to God's, we will not experience true peace and the level of success we would have known had we walked the path He chose. We may make many plans to ensure our success, but the Lord alone causes us to have the victory.

"Suppose one of you wants to build a tower. Will he not first sit down and estimate the cost to see if he has enough money to complete it? For if he lays the foundation and is not able to finish it, everyone who sees it will ridicule him, saying, 'This fellow began to build and was not able to finish.' "Or suppose a king is about to go to war against another king. Will he not first sit down and consider whether he is able with ten thousand men to oppose the one coming against him with twenty thousand? If he is not able, he will send a delegation while the other is still a long way off and will ask for terms of peace. In the same way, any of you who does not give up everything he has cannot be my disciple.

Luke 14:28-33

We should always count the cost before we build on, tear down, modify, or act on any decision. This is the smart thing to do, but we must never leave out Jesus in the process. How can we expect to win the battles of life if we don't first have an accurate battle plan? The problem is, we don't know what the future holds; only God knows. He has been and is there now in our future. He is everywhere at one time—past, present, and future. However, the place that God has for us is in the present, because He said, "I Am." He didn't say, "I was" or "I will be." He said, "I Am."

It is wise to count the cost before making decisions, but we must also remember that the weapons of our warfare are not man-made, but mighty for pulling down strongholds. We can succeed at life, but the choice is up to us. God has given us a free will, but if we choose to follow our own plans, we can't expect Him to just follow along.

This is what the LORD says: Look! I am preparing a disaster for you and devising a plan against you. So turn from your evil ways, each one of you, and reform your ways and your actions.' But they will reply, 'It's no use. We will continue with our own plans; each of us will follow the stubbornness of his evil heart.'

Jeremiah 18:11-12

There are consequences for our actions. If we make evil and greedy plans to the detriment of others, the Lord will avenge them. God is real, and we will reap from the seeds that we sow towards other people. Failure to realize this is a sure plan to fail. God's plan, however, is to give us hope and a future. We just have to turn from our wicked ways and seek Him, and then He will be found by us.

Woe to those who plan iniquity, to those who plot evil on their beds! At morning's light they carry it out because it is in their power to do it. They covet fields and seize them, and houses, and take them. They defraud a man of his home, a fellowman of his inheritance. Therefore, the LORD says: "I am planning disaster against this people, from which you cannot save yourselves.

Micah 2:1-3

It is certain that we will reap a harvest from the seeds we plant. When we make evil plans to bring others down, we, too, will surely be brought down. The disaster is certain, and we will not be able to save ourselves. If we constantly think about what someone else has, then we will covet it and make plans to possess it, even if it is not good for us to have.

Folly delights a man who lacks judgment, but a man of understanding keeps a straight course. Plans fail for lack of counsel, but with many advisers they succeed.

Proverbs 15:21-22

It is always good to seek advice from wise people with expertise in the direction we are considering. It is good to get as much knowledge as possible in making our plans. Making plans without wise advice is just as bad as not making any plans at all. Unwise planning can cause wasted resources and wasted time. Failure to get adequate counsel can lead to discouragement.

Commit to the LORD whatever you do, and your plans will succeed.

Proverbs 16:3

This does not mean we are to give the Lord our list of demands and He will make sure they all come true. If what we desire is best for us according to the plan that He established before we were born, then He will make sure our plans succeed. That is why all plans need to start and end with God.

In his heart a man plans his course, but the LORD determines his steps.

Proverbs 16:9

We may think up many wonderful plans, but ultimately, it is the Lord who decides what happens. We may do things that get us off track, but He is always there to bring us back. Also, we can be so determined to follow our own plans that He lets us do our thing but does not go with us.

Listen to advice and accept instruction, and in the end you will be wise. Many are the plans in a man's heart, but it is the LORD's purpose that prevails.

Proverbs 19:20-21

This Scripture is basically the same as the previous one and many others that we have already studied. It is God who has the plan for our lives, and His purpose for us is best. We have to put our trust in Him and believe. He will lead us into the plan that is best. The key is for us to listen to good advice, accept it, follow it, and gain wisdom from it.

We may have many wonderful plans—and they may all be good plans—but they may not be "God plans." For example, there are many things I would love to do: I would love to learn to play the guitar. I want to be a storyteller. I want to visit nursing homes and have tea parties with some of the residents. I want to write books and poems. I would love to get my master's and doctorate in ministry. I want to be a booster parent in the band for my daughter. I want to have retreats for teenage girls. I feel like I could paint and want to take lessons to learn. And on the list goes. All of these are good ideas, but I can't say that I know God wants me to do all of them. I do feel like a few of these might be in His plan for me, and I definitely know that it is His plan that will prevail. And that is what I want for my life.

Prayer

Prayer is communication between God and us. It consists of both talking and listening. A friendship would not last long if only one person talked and talked and talked and never listened to what the other person had to say. In the God-to-human relationship, it is very important to listen to the One who knows all, sees all, and is everywhere.

We should also realize that God's answer may not always be what we want. Sometimes His answer will be no, and we must trust that He has a very good reason for it. Sometimes we may later see why the answer was no, but sometimes we may never know.

"Whoever would love life and see good days must keep his tongue from evil and his lips from deceitful speech. He must turn from evil and do good; he must seek peace and pursue it. For the eyes of the Lord are on the righteous and his ears are attentive to their prayer, but the face of the Lord is against those who do evil.

1 Peter 3:10 -12

This Scripture tells us one of the keys to having our prayers heard by God: we must keep our mouths from saying evil and deceitful things about others. We must not only make the effort to not do bad things, but we must also intentionally concentrate on doing good things. As long as there is a situation that can be made peaceable between other people and us, we should do what it takes—and that usually means to forgive.

God watches over us to hear our prayers, but that does not mean the answer will always be yes. Sometimes no may be the best answer for us. We will not always understand why we can't have the things we want, but we must develop the confidence that He knows best.

And when you stand praying, if you hold anything against anyone, forgive him, so that your Father in heaven may forgive you your sins.

Mark 11: 25

We cannot approach God with our prayer requests while harboring unforgiveness in our hearts. Unforgiveness makes us unworthy of having our prayers heard. Unforgiveness closes the door, but love opens it wide. When we hold grudges against others, we stand unclean before a holy God. The Lord's Prayer says, "Forgive us our debts as we forgive our debtors." In other words, "Forgive me the things that I have done against You, as I forgive others the things they have done against me."

My prayer is not that you take them out of the world but that you protect them from the evil one.

John 17:15

As we pray for our children, we must realize they will have to go through some hard things in their lives. The thing is, though, we want the Father to be there with them. We can't always be with them, but God can and will. As they go through their issues, we can ask God to strengthen them as He goes with them. Remember, when we say we are going *through* something, which means we are not there to stay. We are going through to the other side, which is the victory!

Brothers, my heart's desire and prayer to God for the Israelites is that they may be saved.

Romans 10:1

Our most important prayer and desire for our children is that they be saved, not only from eternal separation from God, but also from going through all their problems alone. A person's reaction to a situation will determine its outcome. A person's mind-set is a matter of what he or she believes the outcome will be and the confidence of victory on the other side of the problem.

Love must be sincere. Hate what is evil; cling to what is good. Be devoted to one another in brotherly love. Honor one another above yourselves. Never be lacking in zeal, but keep your spiritual fervor, serving the Lord. Be joyful in hope, patient in affliction, faithful in prayer. Share with God's people who are in need. Practice hospitality. Bless those who persecute you; bless and do not curse. Rejoice with those who rejoice; mourn with those who mourn. Live in harmony with one another. Do not be proud, but be willing to associate with people of low position. Do not be conceited. Do not repay anyone evil for evil. Be careful to do what is right in the eyes of everybody. If it is possible, as far as it depends on you, live at peace with everyone. Do not take revenge, my friends, but leave room for God's wrath, for it is written: "It is mine to avenge; I will repay,"

Romans 12:9-19

Buried in this Scripture is the exhortation to be faithful in prayer. However, this nugget is surrounded by encouragement on how to treat others. Loving others is the key to getting our prayers answered. God is all about love, and He cares for us all. But sometimes, purposefully or not, we teach our children to be very selfish. However, we can help both ourselves and others too. "Me, me, me first" is not God's way. As we rely on God to help us help others, He will make sure we are taken care of. Why serve a God that we cannot trust?

Pass the Blessings!

And this is my prayer: that your love may abound more and more in knowledge and depth of insight, so that you may be able to discern what is best and may be pure and blameless until the day of Christ, filled with the fruit of righteousness that comes through Jesus Christ—to the glory and praise of God.

Phillipians 1:9-11

We should pray that our children would be more loving and that they would study and learn more about the needs of others. We should also pray that they would be kind and gentle, receive and give good reports, and be patient with others.

Rejoice in the Lord always. I will say it again: Rejoice! Let your gentleness be evident to all. The Lord is near. Do not be anxious about anything, but in everything, by prayer and petition, with thanksgiving, present your requests to God. And the peace of God, which transcends all understanding, will guard your hearts and your minds in Christ Jesus.

Philippians 4:4-7

Either our children should be taught to pray, or they should be shown how to worry. I say this because we can't do both at the same time. Well, maybe we can try to do both, but our prayers don't leave the room if we're worrying. If we are going to worry and try to figure out our problems and concerns by ourselves, then why bother God with them in the first place? When we pray, we should realize He will work things out for our good if we are living according to His purpose. After we have talked to Him about our concerns, we can thank Him and even rejoice and be at peace. It is important to thank Him for His answer even before we see the result.

Devote yourselves to prayer, being watchful and thankful.

Colossians 4:2

To devote means to set apart for a special purpose, to give ourselves to a specific cause or activity. Our prayers should be taken very seriously as we devote ourselves to a grand cause. Being devoted to something is not a once-in-a-while thing. It must be done often and with concentration on how we can make it better. In praying, we must watch for the answer and thank God for it.

Epaphras, who is one of you and a servant of Christ Jesus, sends greetings. He is always wrestling in prayer for you, that you may stand firm in all the will of God, mature and fully assured.

Colossians 4:12

Our prayers are not a hit-and-miss deal. It is a staying in court and pleading before a righteous judge for the cause of someone else. Our children, our spouses, and others need our continuous prayers. Our prayers help them to stand firm in what God has called them to do. Our prayers will help them to grow up and become more assured of the plans God has for them.

For everything God created is good, and nothing is to be rejected if it is received with thanksgiving, because it is consecrated by the word of God and prayer.

1 Timothy 4:4-5

Our prayers and the Word of God consecrate others when they are willing to accept God's way. None of us are good, and none of us are perfect, but the Word, our prayers, and our faith make all things possible. *To consecrate* something is to cause it to be revered or honored, to devote or dedicate it entirely. Our children and spouses need this from us. We revere and honor them when we pray the Word of God over them. Also, we should make sure to treat them as honorable and revered. God does see them this way. If He didn't, He would not have died for them.

Therefore confess your sins to each other and pray for each other so that you may be healed. The prayer of a righteous man is powerful and effective.

James 5:16

Let's first look at the term *righteous,* which does not imply perfection. Righteousness is perpetual and ongoing. Each day we are being changed to be more like Christ. None of us will reach perfection in Christ here on earth, but we should be moving closer and closer throughout our entire lives.

When our children acknowledge their sins and weaknesses to God and to us, we should not burden them constantly with these facts, but we should pray with them and stay dedicated to them. They may fail, just as we fail in certain areas, but we must stay dedicated in prayer to help them.

For the eyes of the Lord are on the righteous and his ears are attentive to their prayer, but the face of the Lord is against those who do evil."

1 Peter 3:12

God listens to the prayers of those living righteous lives. Being righteous is more than Sunday, going to church and looking holy; Monday, lying about sickness and not going to work; Tuesday, talking about and slandering others; Wednesday, disrespecting bosses and other authorities; Thursday, cursing in traffic; Friday, getting drunk; and Saturday, overspending. God listens to us when we repent, but He knows if we are sincere or if we're just sorry until the next time we do the same thing. God knows and loves us all; however, He is attentive to the prayers of the righteous.

The angel answered, "Your prayers and gifts to the poor have come up as a memorial offering before God.

Acts 10:4

It is good for us to teach our children to be givers and to have active prayer lives, for God remembers all of our actions and gifts as a memorial. A memorial keeps something in remembrance. It is not that God needs something to help Him remember our actions; this Scripture is simply a statement of facts. Our dedication to praying and doing good for the poor are important to God.

When Jesus wanted to know if Peter loved Him, He told him to prove it by feeding His sheep. When we help the poor, it is as though God is setting up a trust fund for us. He remembers the good we do because it would be unjust for Him to forget what we have done for His people.

God is not unjust; he will not forget your work and the love you have shown him as you have helped his people and continue to help them.

Hebrews 6:10

And pray in the Spirit on all occasions with all kinds of prayers and requests. With this in mind, be alert and always keep on praying for all the saints.

Ephesians 6:18

There are many types of prayers. There are on-the-knees prayers, standing-up prayers, lying-on-the-floor prayers, crying prayers, quiet prayers, thought prayers, laughing prayers, at-work prayers, at-church prayers, in-the-grocery-store prayers, driving prayers, formal and informal prayers, cleaning-the-house prayers, and many other kinds. The point is, praying is a continuous and constant conversation with God. This does not have to interrupt our daily living, for God wants us to render the proper respect, time, and attention due to our employers, schools, and families.

For this reason, since the day we heard about you, we have not stopped praying for you and asking God to fill you with the knowledge of his will through all spiritual wisdom and understanding. And we pray this in order that you may live a life worthy of the Lord and may please him in every way: bearing fruit in every good work, growing in the knowledge of God, being strengthened with all power according to his glorious might so that you may have great endurance and patience, and joyfully giving thanks to the Father, who has qualified you to share in the inheritance of the saints in the kingdom of light. For he has rescued us from the dominion of darkness and brought us into the kingdom of the Son he loves, in whom we have redemption, the forgiveness of sins.

Colossians 1:9-14

I have been blessed with a praying mother, a praying grandmother, a praying grandfather, praying aunts, praying sisters, and many other praying relatives. I have seen the power of prayer change things. Because of prayer, I've seen healings, I've experienced protection, I've been given ideas, I've been rebuked, I've been given the answer no, and I've received love and strength. I've grown through prayer. Prayers are not just about our talking to God, but prayer is about our waiting to hear what He has to say to us. He does have something to say.

Forgive—For Your sake, Let it Go!

But Joseph said to them, "Don't be afraid. Am I in the place of God? 20You intended to harm me, but God intended it for good to accomplish what is now being done, the saving of many lives. 21So then, don't be afraid. I will provide for you and your children." And he reassured them and spoke kindly to them.

Genesis 50:19-21

Joseph's brothers resented him and sold him into slavery when he was young. He was later put into prison for something he did not do and forgotten by someone who had promised to help free him. But despite everything Joseph went through, he did not let himself get bitter; bitterness and unforgiveness would only have destroyed him.

God had a plan for Joseph's life before he was ever sold into slavery and before he ever went to prison. That plan was still going to happen regardless of whatever else happened in Joseph's life or the number of years that passed. When Joseph saw his brothers again after so many years, he spoke kindly to them. If we have truly forgiven others, there will be outward signs of it. We can be kind, and it will truly come from the heart.

Forgive us our debts, as we also have forgiven our debtor.

Matthew 6:12

If it is our desire for God to forgive us, then it is absolutely necessary for us to forgive others. To the measure that we forgive, we will be forgiven. Traveling beside the road of our forgiveness in Christ is our forgiveness of others. Also, stopped at the pothole in the road of life is our unforgiveness towards others, which is directly related to the level of forgiveness we will receive.

For if you forgive men when they sin against you, your heavenly Father will also forgive you. But if you do not forgive men their sins, your Father will not forgive your sins.

Matthew 6:14-15

And when you stand praying, if you hold anything against anyone, forgive him, so that your Father in heaven may forgive you your sins.

Mark 11:25

"Do not judge, and you will not be judged. Do not condemn, and you will not be condemned. Forgive, and you will be forgiven.

Luke 6:37

And with that he breathed on them and said, "Receive the Holy Spirit. 23If you forgive anyone his sins, they are forgiven; if you do not forgive them, they are not forgiven."

John 20:22

We are instructed to forgive, and when we do not, we are rebelling against God. This is so important for us to model to our kids. As it becomes more of a part of our lives, it will be easier for our children to imitate us and make it part of their lives.

The Scriptures above are very simple and straightforward. Unforgiveness hinders our prayers and ability to receive forgiveness. Actions and reactions are listed in one Scripture. If we judge others ("They don't need to do that"), then more scrutiny will be directed towards our actions. If we condemn ("I hope they get what they deserve"), then we will reap judgment just as severe or even more so. However, if we forgive ("Maybe they didn't mean what they said [or did]"), we will be forgiven for what we do or say. By our actions, we trigger things in the spiritual world and determine outcomes.

Then Peter came to Jesus and asked, "Lord, how many times shall I forgive my brother when he sins against me? Up to seven times?" Jesus answered, "I tell you, not seven times, but seventy-seven times. "Therefore, the kingdom of heaven is like a king who wanted to settle accounts with his servants. As he began the settlement, a man who owed him ten thousand talents was brought to him. Since he was not able to pay, the master ordered that he and his wife and his children and all that he had be sold to repay the debt. "The servant fell on his knees before him. 'Be patient with me,' he begged, 'and I will pay back everything.' The servant's master took pity on him, canceled the debt and let him go. "But when that servant went out, he found one of his fellow servants who owed him a hundred denarii. He grabbed him and began to choke him. 'Pay back what you owe me!' he demanded. "His fellow servant fell to his knees and begged him, 'Be patient with me, and I will pay you back.' "But he refused. Instead, he went off and had the man thrown into prison until he could pay the debt. When the other servants saw what had happened, they were greatly distressed and went and told their master everything that had happened. "Then the master called the servant in. 'You wicked servant,' he said, 'I canceled all that debt of yours because you begged me to. Shouldn't you have had mercy on your fellow servant just as I had on you?' In anger his master turned him over to the jailers to be tortured, until he should pay back all he owed. "This is how my heavenly Father will treat each of you unless you forgive your brother from your heart."

Matthew 18:21-35

This verse says we must forgive seventy-seven times. If a person kept track of the number of times he or she had forgiven someone, and on the seventy-eighth time said, "Aha, I don't have to forgive you anymore, for you have exceeded the forgiveness that you were allotted," then that person has totally missed the point. In actuality, a forgiving heart is not present at all because the individual was keeping a record of all the wrongs done by the other person.

But what if God treated us this way? Countless times a day, we need His forgiveness, and as soon as we ask for it, He grants it immediately. He has to do this in order to be able to tolerate us. If He did not forgive us immediately, then we would not be able to stand in His presence. The act would still be there because it is not washed away until it is forgiven.

It is amazing the level of understanding we want from others concerning our issues while we are not nearly as understanding of others and their issues. The funny thing is, our issues are probably worse than theirs. We sometimes hold on to unforgiveness with our kids when they don't do the things we want them to do. It is amazing how long we can hold on to a grudge and be proud of every year it lingers: "They hurt me, and I'm not letting them go." The same thing applies for kids toward their parents.

Yes, we've all been hurt. I've hurt my kids, and I've been hurt by my mother. I will apologize to my kids until the day I die because I want them to have resolution. My mother has apologized for some things, but I have had to just release other issues for my own sake. I can't and won't let unforgiveness stop me.

I had a relative that was not nice to me for years; they would talk about my mother and sister to their daughters and others in a room nearby, intending for me to hear them. They also did many other things that I don't mention. What's the use in that? But at the end of their life, God made it possible for me to be with them and help them before they passed away. God is good!

So watch yourselves. "If your brother sins, rebuke him, and if he repents, forgive him. If he sins against you seven times in a day, and seven times comes back to you and says, 'I repent,' forgive him." The apostles said to the Lord, "Increase our faith!"

Luke 17:3-5

This is not an easy task! Immediately after Jesus made this statement about forgiving many times in a day, the disciples asked for more faith. Basically, they were saying, "Lord, You are going to have to help me with this! Help me, and give me strength." Though they recognized the enormity of the task, they did not back away from the challenge. We will definitely have to pray to fulfill the forgiveness command when someone is constantly irritating us. But Jesus would not have given us the directive if it were impossible to do. Remember, all things are possible with God.

Jesus said, "Father, forgive them, for they do not know what they are doing."

Luke 23:34

As hard as it may seem, some people do not realize what they are doing to us. Others may know what they are doing but don't understand the far-reaching consequences of their behavior. Hopefully, by this point in the chapter, we have realized what our lack of forgiveness does to us as well as to others.

Repent of this wickedness and pray to the Lord. Perhaps he will forgive you for having such a thought in your heart. For I see that you are full of bitterness and captive to sin."

Acts 8:22-23

Even our thoughts must be repented of and forgiveness sought. We can tell when others are bitter about something, and when we see this going on in our children, it is good to talk with them and discuss the necessity of getting rid of the bitterness. Thoughts lead to actions. Other Scriptures say if we dwell on certain thoughts, then it's the same as if we had actually done them.

The punishment inflicted on him by the majority is sufficient for him. Now instead, you ought to forgive and comfort him, so that he will not be overwhelmed by excessive sorrow. I urge you, therefore, to reaffirm your love for him.

2 Corinthians 2:6-8

Once we have disciplined our children, then it is time to receive them in love. Under the weight of excessive punishment and disapproval, a child may make a bad choice at a critical fork in the road. It is always good to explain to children that we don't like what they did, but we do love them always. In love, it is good for children to suffer the consequences of their actions, but our love and forgiveness for them must remain constant.

Bear with each other and forgive whatever grievances you may have against one another. Forgive as the Lord forgave you. And over all these virtues put on love, which binds them all together in perfect unity.

Colossians 3:13-14

I don't believe anything worse could be done to us than what has already been done to God. Yet He forgives us daily for all our sins and transgressions. He knows us completely but loves us anyway. He knows we are human, and we must remember that others are human as well. Forgiveness is still required in our relationships with them. Love is still required.

This is hard stuff, I know, but I want to go to higher levels in Christ. I'm not saying I have mastered this—because I have not—but I am saying what the Bible says on the subject. I earnestly desire in my heart to be this way. Some days I am more successful at it than I am on other days.

So let's do this together. You pray for my strength and faith, and I will pray for yours. I will pray for everyone who reads this book that God will grant extra strength to accomplish His Word and pass on the blessing of a forgiving life to his or her kids.

For I will forgive their wickedness and will remember their sins no more."

Hebrews 8:8:12

That's a tall order, but remember, He does not remember our sins after He has forgiven them. There are, of course, consequences for sin; however, He does not keep a record of our sins when we ask for forgiveness. He never says, "Yeah, yeah, yeah, you said you were sorry for doing this same thing twenty-five times ago." He lets it go!

Praise the LORD, O my soul, and forget not all his benefits— who forgives all your sins and heals all your diseases,

Psalms 103:2-3

Which is easier: to say, 'Your sins are forgiven,' or to say, 'Get up and walk'?

Matthew 9:5

Which is easier: to say to the paralytic, 'Your sins are forgiven,' or to say, 'Get up, take your mat and walk'? But that you may know that the Son of Man has authority on earth to forgive sins . . . ." He said to the paralytic, "I tell you, get up, take your mat and go home."

Mark 2:9-11

Which is easier: to say, 'Your sins are forgiven,' or to say, 'Get up and walk'? But that you may know that the Son of Man has authority on earth to forgive sins.

Luke 5:23-24

Is any one of you sick? He should call the elders of the church to pray over him and anoint him with oil in the name of the Lord. And the prayer offered in faith will make the sick person well; the Lord will raise him up. If he has sinned, he will be forgiven. Therefore confess your sins to each other and pray for each other so that you may be healed.

James 5:14-16

These five Scriptures support the statement that some illnesses are related to unforgiveness held towards others. Matthew, Mark, and Luke told the same story about Jesus and the paralytic and recorded Jesus' statement on forgiveness of sin and healing. In fact, their stories are practically interchangeable!

Unforgiveness can affect our physical bodies and cause serious sickness. It is similar to wanting to poison someone but drinking the poison ourselves. Unforgiveness affects us mentally because our minds are constantly dwelling on those thoughts. Our thoughts then affect our actions. We refuse to treat others right because of the bitterness that unforgiveness has invited along for the ride. It affects us physically, mentally, and socially, and the doctor's visit will affect us monetarily. So let's just let it go! It's too heavy to carry, and we were not built to carry that burden anyway.

I have family members who called me and my siblings "bastards" and other such names. We were looked down upon by many people, though God did provide several people to build us up. Several relatives thought that none of us would amount to anything—and said so. Coming from relatives, these words exacted a much deeper hurt than if they had come from someone else.

But God had a plan for our lives, and He worked all things out despite the many stumbling blocks placed before us. All my siblings survived and are doing well. Five of my sisters hold degrees and work in good occupations. One is an English teacher with a master's degree, another is a social worker with a bachelor's, and another is a social worker, counselor, and advocate with several degrees. Still another sister is a chemical engineer and project manager, while another works in accounting with her bachelor's degree. I myself have a bachelor's in ministry.

For twenty years, another sister has been on her job working with troubled kids and is helping to raise three small foster kids. My brother is now a photographer and returning back to school to get a degree. Five of us have been married from ten to more than thirty years. My God is good. All of us survived the bad talk and criticism, and I think it is because my mother taught us love and forgiveness. She was mistreated also, but she continued in relationship with these people and forgave them.

Loving God, Loving Others

If I speak in the tongues of men and of angels, but have not love, I am only a resounding gong or a clanging cymbal. If I have the gift of prophecy and can fathom all mysteries and all knowledge, and if I have a faith that can move mountains, but have not love, I am nothing. If I give all I possess to the poor and surrender my body to the flames, but have not love, I gain nothing. Love is patient, love is kind. It does not envy, it does not boast, it is not proud. It is not rude, it is not self-seeking, it is not easily angered, it keeps no record of wrongs. Love does not delight in evil but rejoices with the truth. It always protects, always trusts, always hopes, always perseveres.

1Corinthians 13:1-7

Loving others is so important to God. He commands us to love others as ourselves. This command is second only to loving God Himself. If we love God and others, we can live victoriously in every aspect of our lives. If we are the best speakers in the world but don't love others, it is useless. If we know the future and are very intelligent and can figure out deep mysteries but have not love for others, then it means nothing. If we are congressional representatives or senators but have not love, we are nothing. If we are people of great faith and give all our wealth to the poor, our actions are useless without love; and even if we are martyred for our beliefs but do not love people, it means nothing.

When we truly love, we are patient with people and kind to all. We neither desire nor take others' possessions. We don't brag about our abilities, and we don't flaunt them before others to make them jealous. We are not rude, and we don't insist on our own way. We may get angry, but only for a good cause that glorifies God and benefits others, and we do not stay angry for hours. We don't keep rehearsing before others the wrongs and mistakes they have done. We are not happy when others make mistakes or fail at something. Love is protective; it trusts and hopes, and it doesn't give up on others.

This is a hard Scripture to break down, because I fail in so many ways, but let me try to explain the love I show to my family and the areas where I struggle. I want to do better, and that begins with my husband and children. If I love my husband and kids, why am I sometimes rude and disrespectful to them? I can be unkind at times; I get angry and bring up the past before them. I want my own way a good bit of the time because, you know, I'm sure I have the best plan. On the other hand, I would give anything and everything to help my family, and I would die for them. I would never flaunt my abilities before them to make them feel small. I don't rejoice when they make mistakes.

However, I used to get mad and stay that way for days. I made the whole house miserable, and I gloated over the power that I had, but now, as I look back, I am so embarrassed over my behavior. It is a bad thing to say about your home that when Mama is not happy, then no one is happy. As mothers, we must recognize the power in this statement and use it for good influence with our kids. We have the ability to set the course for their entire lives. Do we really want to set the course for a life of negativity? The things we do to them will surely be passed on to our grandkids. Do we really want the actions of today to be our regrets of tomorrow for the next generation? Our innocent grandkids will receive the consequences from what we put into our kids today. Oh, God, help me to realize the blessing that has been entrusted to me and to do only good for my children. Help me to be like You and act like You and love like You. As long as I do my part with Your help, then I have done all that I can do, but the final decisions will be my children's choices.

Parents are thought of as mothers and fathers who would give the shirts off their backs and die for their beliefs, but if their families do not recognize these traits in them, then what have they accomplished? What if their children would say, "Yes, but you don't know the whole story about my parents. They don't give me love and forgiveness. They are just plain hard!" Our public selves must align with our private selves. The way we treat our families is very important because they are the ones who live with us and know the smallest details about our lives.

He who covers over an offense promotes love, but whoever repeats the matter separates close friends.

Proverbs 17:9

It is not always necessary to broadcast our children's wrongs. At times, they will make childish mistakes, just as we occasionally make mistakes. We don't want everyone to know all of our mistakes; we hope someone will give us a break. Our children want the same thing and need the same treatment from us. When they do wrong, we should discuss the matter with them privately and administer any appropriate consequences.

"You have heard that it was said, 'Love your neighbor and hate your enemy.' But I tell you: Love your enemies and pray for those who persecute you, that you may be sons of your Father in heaven. He causes his sun to rise on the evil and the good, and sends rain on the righteous and the unrighteous. If you love those who love you, what reward will you get? Are not even the tax collectors doing that? And if you greet only your brothers, what are you doing more than others? Do not even pagans do that? Be perfect, therefore, as your heavenly Father is perfect.

Matthews 5:43-48

If we love only the people who love us and are good to us, then we are not mature. God does not give sunshiny days to good people and rainy days to bad ones. There is no reward for us if we are good to only friends and family. Yes, we should be good to the ones we love, but we must stretch ourselves to reach out to others that are no relation to us, to those we don't even know or like. The challenge is to be perfect in our love towards others, just as the Father is perfect in His love for us. He loved us before we knew Him, He loves us when we deny Him, He loves us when we don't obey Him, and He loves us when we decide He does not exist or that we don't need Him. His love is perfect and complete, and we should strive to imitate Him.

Because of the increase of wickedness, the love of most will grow cold.

Matthew 24: 12

It is amazing how we imitate others. The more we expose ourselves to others' actions, the more we excuse their actions as just the way they are. But what if we exposed ourselves to more loving and giving people? Might we become more loving and giving? Wickedness is so prevalent, and there are so many ways that people can harm others. When we are wicked and do not care about others' feelings, then we are not able to be loving. Night and day can't coexist, good and bad can't coexist, and being loving and being wicked can't coexist.

"The most important one," answered Jesus, "is this: 'Hear, O Israel, the Lord our God, the Lord is one. Love the Lord your God with all your heart and with all your soul and with all your mind and with all your strength.' The second is this: 'Love your neighbor as yourself.' There is no commandment greater than these." "Well said, teacher," the man replied. "You are right in saying that God is one and there is no other but him. To love him with all your heart, with all your understanding and with all your strength, and to love your neighbor as yourself is more important than all burnt offerings and sacrifices."

Mark 12:29-33

We cannot love God in part; our true love for Him can be expressed only in the whole, through the mind, the body, and the soul. Giving to the poor, volunteering, attending church, and other religious acts mean nothing if the love of God is not in our hearts. I believe if our kids see us actively loving others, they will be more likely to show love to others.

"But I tell you who hear me: Love your enemies, do good to those who hate you, bless those who curse you, pray for those who mistreat you. If someone strikes you on one cheek, turn to him the other also. If someone takes your cloak, do not stop him from taking your tunic. Give to everyone who asks you, and if anyone takes

what belongs to you, do not demand it back. Do to others as you would have them do to you.

Luke 6:27-31

I must admit, this is a very demanding Scripture. It takes a very mature Christian to fulfill these requirements. I hope to be there in my lifetime, but I must admit that I am not there yet. I do understand that it is not the people who wrong us that we should hate, but the action displayed. I understand that sometimes they may have yielded to the temptation of satan or to their flesh. Regardless of how the action came forth, such people are separated from the love of God and need to be shown God's loving and forgiving ways.

"If you love those who love you, what credit is that to you? Even 'sinners' love those who love them. And if you do good to those who are good to you, what credit is that to you? Even 'sinners' do that. And if you lend to those from whom you expect repayment, what credit is that to you? Even 'sinners' lend to 'sinners,' expecting to be repaid in full. But love your enemies, do good to them, and lend to them without expecting to get anything back. Then your reward will be great, and you will be sons of the Most High, because he is kind to the ungrateful and wicked. Be merciful, just as your Father is merciful.

Luke 6:32-36

Loving others is so important to God. It does not matter if the person is a friend, a family member, or an enemy. He simply wants us to be kind and treat others with love. He wants us to do this with no expectation of repayment or reward here on earth. Our repayment will come from God.

It would be so good if we did things with no expectation of repayment, if we just did good for the sake of doing good. Nike's slogan is "Just do it." What if we just did it? God does many things for us just because He loves us, and there is really nothing we can give back to Him. He does it because He loves us, and that's how we need to be with others.

It was just before the Passover Feast. Jesus knew that the time had come for him to leave this world and go to the Father. Having loved his own who were in the world, he now showed them the full extent of his love.

John 13:1

Jesus' love for us was fully revealed when He died on the cross. He made the ultimate sacrifice with His life. I wonder to what degree we love others. What are we willing to sacrifice for the good of someone else? We would sacrifice for a family member, or maybe even for a friend, but what about a stranger, someone totally different from us?

The love that Jesus has for us is so profoundly full and perfect. He is not necessarily asking us to die for someone else, but can we give up some of our planned money for the needs of someone else? Can we forgo that planned shopping trip, vacation, expensive car, or second home? I'm not saying any of these things are necessarily wrong, but I am saying it would be good to use our prosperity to bless others.

The evening meal was being served, and the devil had already prompted Judas Iscariot, son of Simon, to betray Jesus. Jesus knew that the Father had put all things under his power, and that he had come from God and was returning to God; so he got up from the meal, took off his outer clothing, and wrapped a towel around his waist. After that, he poured water into a basin and began to wash his disciples' feet, drying them with the towel that was wrapped around him.

John 13:2-5

Amazingly, even though Jesus knew Judas had already betrayed Him, He still washed his feet. He performed the ultimate and lowest act of a servant for a man who was about to turn Him over to the authorities to be beaten and crucified. When we are persuaded by greed to hurt or neglect others, how can we say that we love the Father?

"A new command I give you: Love one another. As I have loved you, so you must love one another. By this all men will know that you are my disciples, if you love one another."

John 13:34-35

Take note of the strong verb used when Jesus says we must love one another. He didn't ask if we would mind, or if we could, or that it would be good to do. That must mean that we have to love others and there is no alternative. I love my siblings, but some of them do things that I don't like. I love my children, but I don't always like all of the things they do. God loves me, but I know He does not like a lot of my behavior. Loving others proves that I belong to God, and He enables me to love others.

"If you love me, you will obey what I command. And I will ask the Father, and he will give you another Counselor to be with you forever— the Spirit of truth. The world cannot accept him, because it neither sees him nor knows him. But you know him, for he lives with you and will be in you. I will not leave you as orphans; I will come to you. Before long, the world will not see me anymore, but you will see me. Because I live, you also will live. On that day you will realize that I am in my Father, and you are in me, and I am in you. Whoever has my commands and obeys them, he is the one who loves me. He who loves me will be loved by my Father, and

I too will love him and show myself to him.": Jesus replied, "If anyone loves me, he will obey my teaching. My Father will love him, and we will come to him and make our home with him. He who does not love me will not obey my teaching. These words you hear are not my own; they belong to the Father who sent me.

John 14:15-24

Obeying God and loving God go hand in hand. We demonstrate our love for God by obeying Him. He wants us to love Him with all our hearts and love others as ourselves. In obeying these two commands, we obey all others in the process. God loves us and wants our obedience for our own good. Protection and joy are found in our obedience to Him, and our obedience invites His presence into our lives.

"As the Father has loved me, so have I loved you. Now remain in my love. If you obey my commands, you will remain in my love, just as I have obeyed my Father's commands and remain in his love. I have told you this so that my joy may be in you and that your joy may be complete. My command is this: Love each other as I have loved you. Greater love has no one than this, that he lay down his life for his friends. You are my friends if you do what I command. I no longer call you servants, because a servant does not know his master's business. Instead, I have called you friends, for everything that I learned from my Father I have made known to you. You did not choose me, but I chose you and appointed you to go and bear fruit—fruit

that will last. Then the Father will give you whatever you ask in my name. This is my command: Love each other.

John 15:9 -17

This is a command to love.

When they had finished eating, Jesus said to Simon Peter, "Simon son of John, do you truly love me more than these?" "Yes, Lord," he said, "you know that I love you." Jesus said, "Feed my lambs.": Again Jesus said, "Simon son of John, do you truly love me?" He answered, "Yes, Lord, you know that I love you." Jesus said, "Take care of my sheep.": The third time he said to him, "Simon son of John, do you love me?" Peter was hurt because Jesus asked him the third time, "Do you love me?" He said, "Lord, you know all things; you know that I love you. Jesus said, "Feed my sheep.

John 21:15 -17

In God's eyes, doing is an expression of loving. Saying that we love others is not enough; we have to demonstrate that love. Taking care of the basic needs of others is love. If we have the ability to take care of a need, then we should do so. In fact, the need was shown to us so that we could partake in the blessing of fulfilling the prayer or desire of the person.

You see, at just the right time, when we were still powerless, Christ died for the ungodly. Very rarely will anyone die for a righteous man, though for a good man someone might possibly dare to die. But God demonstrates his own love for us in this: while we were still sinners, Christ died for us.

Romans 5:6-8

When we were still enemies of God, we didn't know Him or didn't care to know Him. Yet Jesus died for us anyway because of His love for us. He set an example for us to follow in caring for those we know and don't know, and for those who love us and those who don't. His love is different from what we call love, but it is the kind of love we should aspire to display before the world, for they will know we are His through this demonstration of love.

And we know that in all things God works for the good of those who love him, who have been called according to his purpose

Romans 8:2

Let no debt remain outstanding, except the continuing debt to love one another, for he who loves his fellowman has fulfilled the law. The commandments, "Do not commit adultery," "Do not murder," "Do not steal," "Do not covet," and whatever other commandment there may be, are summed up in this one rule: "Love your neighbor as yourself." Love does no harm to its neighbor. Therefore love is the fulfillment of the law.

Romans 13:8-10

It is the Law that we should love others. We are in debt and the only way to pay that debt is to love others, Love seeks the best for others. It wants others to receive good just as we receive that which is good.

Be on your guard; stand firm in the faith; be men of courage; be strong. Do everything in love.

1Corinthians 16:13-14

Let me repeat that: all that we do should be done in love and with love. To do this requires us to be on guard and watchful. We have to make the decision to love and then be firm and dedicated to that decision. Courage and strength can help us to be successful in walking in love. It is not an easy decision, but it is a mandate from our Father.

If anyone has caused grief, he has not so much grieved me as he has grieved all of you, to some extent—not to put it too severely. The punishment inflicted on him by the majority is sufficient for him. Now instead, you ought to forgive and comfort him, so that he will not be overwhelmed by excessive sorrow. I urge you, therefore, to reaffirm your love for him.

2Corinthians 2:5-8

After someone has been punished and suffered the consequences of wrong behavior, we need to show love to the individual. In the case of parents, I am speaking about our children. Yes, they must be punished at times because they will do things that require punishment, but we have to love them out of their sorrow. If we leave them there, they may take a different road from the one they would normally take.

We have all made decisions in anger and in the heat of the moment, but children, because of their immaturity, are more likely to react and make things worse. We should explain to them why their actions were wrong and let them know the reason for the next step we must take with them. Then, after the punishment, comfort and love must be freely given. They should never be withheld as part of the punishment. Nothing can separate us from the love of Christ, and nothing should separate our love from our children. We may not always like them, but we should always love them.

I am not commanding you, but I want to test the sincerity of your love by comparing it with the earnestness of others. For you know the grace of our Lord Jesus Christ, that though he was rich, yet for your sakes he became poor, so that you through his poverty might become rich.

2 Corinthians 8:8-9

The love of God is vastly different from the human definition of love. Our love is so selfish and self-centered. It gives only after it has figured out what it will get back. But real love freely gives and gives. Christ gave up the pleasures of heaven for a while to come to earth to purchase our freedom from sin. We have nothing to give in payment; we cannot pay that price, for it is too high. But God does not expect us to do so; His love is sacrificial, and He has already paid the price. Sometimes we have to offer a sacrifice of love for others. In having children, we have made the decision to be somewhat poorer because kids cost money and require a large investment of time.

You, my brothers, were called to be free. But do not use your freedom to indulge the sinful nature; rather, serve one another in love. The entire law is summed up in a single command: "Love your neighbor as yourself." If you keep on biting and devouring each other, watch out or you will be destroyed by each other.

Galatians 5:13-15

We should do nothing that causes someone else to become discouraged. Everything we do should aid someone else to do better. When we treat others mean, we teach them how to be mean, and that meanness will eventually make its way back to us. We may think it makes us feel better to think of hateful ways to treat people, but in reality, when we purposefully do things in an unloving way, we hurt ourselves as well as others.

For this reason I kneel before the Father, from whom his whole family in heaven and on earth derives its name. I pray that out of his glorious riches he may strengthen you with power through his Spirit in your inner being, so that Christ may dwell in your hearts through faith. And I pray that you, being rooted and established in love, may have power, together with all the saints, to grasp how wide and long and high and deep is the love of Christ, and to know this love that surpasses knowledge—that you may be filled to the measure of all the fullness of God.

Ephesians 3:14 -15

Our human knowledge cannot explain the dimensions of the love of God. It is too long, too wide, too high, and too deep. We cannot explain its actions, nor can we explain its lack of action on some issues. Our total and complete trust in Him will have to be enough.

Pass the Blessings!

As a prisoner for the Lord, then, I urge you to live a life worthy of the calling you have received. Be completely humble and gentle; be patient, bearing with one another in love. Make every effort to keep the unity of the Spirit through the bond of peace. There is one body and one Spirit— just as you were called to one hope when you were called— one Lord, one faith, one baptism; one God and Father of all, who is over all and through all and in all.

Ephesians 4:1-6

Believers are one, having the same Creator, and God sees us as one. We are His children, and it really hurts Him when we don't look after one another. Basically, when we don't love others, we can't say that we love God, because His creations, in a sense, are part of Him. I didn't create my kids, but I take it personally when they are mistreated by someone else. If I create a piece of art, sew something, or bake a cake, I don't want to hear bad comments about it.

Be imitators of God, therefore, as dearly loved children and live a life of love, just as Christ loved us and gave himself up for us as a fragrant offering and sacrifice to God.

Ephesians 5:1-2

We shouldn't just do loving things; we are to live a life of love. This type of love is sacrificial as a lifestyle. This type of life looks to see what it can do to help someone else. The appetite of this type of love is satisfied only when it helps others; it starves when it does not.

If you have any encouragement from being united with Christ, if any comfort from his love, if any fellowship with the Spirit, if any tenderness and compassion, then make my joy complete by being like-minded, having the same love, being one in spirit and purpose. Do nothing out of selfish ambition or vain conceit, but in humility consider others better than yourselves. Each of you should look not only to your own interests, but also to the interests of others.

Philippians 2:1-4

In this "me, me, me" world that we live in, this is a tall order. However, it is a Christ order for us to live by and direct towards others. He will take care of us if we take care of others. It really is a matter of trust in Christ, knowing He will do and perform as He says He will.

We should not perform good deeds just so others will know about them and think we are good. It can't be a publicly staged performance, like having an article printed in the newspaper. We can do so much if we don't mind who gets the credit.

Some people are not capable of taking care of their interests. Some don't know the things they are entitled to, and we who have the knowledge should help them. This world was not meant to be an "I got mine and now you get yours" society. We are to share with others the same encouragement, comfort, fellowship, tenderness, and compassion that we have received from the Father. In the next Scripture, we will see that we are to clothe ourselves with these qualities.

Therefore, as God's chosen people, holy and dearly loved, clothe yourselves with compassion, kindness, humility, gentleness and patience.

Colossians 3:12

May the Lord make your love increase and overflow for each other and for everyone else, just as ours does for you. 13 May he strengthen your hearts so that you will be blameless and holy in the presence of our God and Father when our Lord Jesus comes with all his holy ones.

1 Thessalonians 3:12-13

Our love for others should grow to the point that it overflows from us onto others. This love can be realized only through the strengthening of the Lord. Again, it is not going to be easy, but it is doable. He will never ask us to do something that

He knows we cannot do; He is not a tease. Through the might and power of the Holy Spirit, we can love like He wants us to love.

God is not unjust; he will not forget your work and the love you have shown him as you have helped his people and continue to help them.

Hebrews 6:10

It would be unjust for God to not take care of our needs as we take care of others. I am not saying not to pay your bills, because that would be irresponsible. We should definitely take care of our responsibilities, but because God has blessed us, we can afford to help other people too. We can bless people at times other than Christmas and Thanksgiving. We should make it a lifestyle to be helpful to others. We are not expected to help everyone, and we may not be able to give in the same way that someone else can, but we can all do something.

Let us hold unswervingly to the hope we profess, for he who promised is faithful. And let us consider how we may spur one another on toward love and good deeds.

Hebrews 10: 23-24

Once we have adapted our lives to being helpful, we can help others to become givers also.

Above all, love each other deeply, because love covers over a multitude of sins. Offer hospitality to one another without grumbling. Each one should use whatever gift he has received to serve others, faithfully administering God's grace in its various forms. If anyone speaks, he should do it as one speaking the very words of God. If anyone serves, he should do it with the strength God provides, so that in all things God may be praised through Jesus Christ.

1 Peter 4:8-11

When our love is deeply rooted in God, it becomes more like the love that God has for us. We will cover others as we want to be covered. We won't just make excuses for those with the same problems as ours. When we do this, we are often making excuses for our own shortcomings. We are somehow making things all right for ourselves.

Whatever God blesses us with, we are supposed to share with others. When we speak, we should represent Christ and do it with love and kindness. Serving and giving are traits that require the help and strength of God. This type of life is not easy to live, and many will not want it because of the selfishness in their hearts.

Do not love the world or anything in the world. If anyone loves the world, the love of the Father is not in him. For everything in the world—the cravings of sinful man, the lust of his eyes and the boasting of what he has and does—comes not from the

Father but from the world. The world and its desires pass away, but the man who does the will of God lives forever.

1 John 2:15 -17

As a society, we value things more than we value people. The Bible does not say that we can't have some things, but if it's a choice between feeding or helping someone and getting another or better something, which is better? The cravings (not the needs) of man, the things our eyes see and decide that we must have, and the boasting that we are independent, self-made people are all vain and prideful notions that come from the world's point of view, not God's. We have nothing that was not given to us, nor can we do anything that God does not allow (not necessarily approve of) us to do. So if I see the need of a brother but choose to take care of my own selfish wants, that is not the love of God.

The funny thing is that when I do give to others, God often blesses me with many of the things that I wanted and at a fraction of the cost. Or sometimes the item will be given to me by someone who didn't know that I wanted it. For example, at this moment in my life, I am planning a graduation party for my son and getting together all the things he needs for college in the fall. I am working on getting my book published, and things in my house need attention. My daughter has her needs, and I want to do something for my husband, who was recently promoted to manager. My older son's car needs repairs, and we have two Westie puppies that need attention. All of this is on top of our mortgage payment and other bills, the cost of music lessons, and the expenses of doctor bills.

With all this going on, I decided I wanted to change my bedroom to a deep red and brownish-gold color. I wanted a duvet so that I would not have to change everything when the seasons changed. I found the exact thing I wanted, along with two pillow shams in the exact color I wanted, in a local thrift store. Since then, in other thrift stores, I found a pair of lace curtains that fit perfectly the long, somewhat thin windows in my room. Also, I found some fabric that was perfect for some pillows I wanted to make, and I found a small loveseat that I wanted to cover.

Speaking of the loveseat, I wanted to place it at the foot of my bed, so there were certain qualifications it needed to meet. Furthermore, I did not want to spend more than twenty-five to thirty dollars. My sister took me to a thrift store that had a loveseat small enough to fit at the bottom of my bed. I also have two ottomans on either side of the loveseat; these open up and provide storage, but they also make great tables. Both of these were found at another thrift store.

Jo-Ann, a fabric store, had a sale on material that was the exact color of fabric in my living room and dining room. Also, a Walmart near me was getting rid of their fabric department and all cut items were 75 percent off. Not only did I get the fabric I wanted at a great price, but I was also able to add fringe and embellish my chair covers, curtains, and pillows.

I wanted a small table for a desk in my bedroom, and I found one with the exact measurements needed to fit near my window in my bedroom. Also, during this time, Kohl's sent me five or six ten-dollars-off coupons; JCPenney sent me one ten-dollar coupon; Bed Bath & Beyond sent me two five-dollars-off coupons; I received two or three Belk's five-dollars-off coupons; and Copeland's and Friday's sent meal coupons for buying one meal and getting one free.

I am an accessory queen, and I cannot count the many times I have found items that matched perfectly, had items given to me, or found accessories at a thrift store. I have a sister, Linitia, who listens and blesses me often with many wonderful things. I try to be a blessing to her also.

God has blessed me in so many ways as I have opened my purse to be a blessing to others who could not provide for some of their basic needs. I do love some things, but I love the Lord more, and as I take care of others, He takes care of me.

This is how we know who the children of God are and who the children of the devil are: Anyone who does not do what is right is not a child of God; nor is anyone who does not love his brother. This is the message you heard from the beginning: We should love one another. Do not be like Cain, who belonged to the evil one and murdered his brother. And why did he murder him? Because his own actions were evil and his brother's were righteous. Do not be surprised, my brothers, if the world hates you. We know that we have passed from death to life, because we love our brothers. Anyone who does not love remains in death. Anyone who hates his brother is a murderer, and you know that no murderer has eternal life in him. This is how we know what love is: Jesus Christ laid down his life for us. And we ought to lay down our lives for our brothers. If anyone has material possessions and sees his brother in need but has no pity on him, how can the love of God be in him? Dear children, let us not love with words or tongue but with actions and in truth. This then is how we know that we belong to the truth, and how we set our hearts at rest in his presence whenever our hearts condemn us:

1 John 3:10-20

Dear friends, let us love one another, for love comes from God. Everyone who loves has been born of God and knows God. Whoever does not love does not know God, because God is love. This is how God showed his love among us: He sent his one and only Son into the world that we might live through him. This is love: not that we loved God, but that he loved us and sent his Son as an atoning sacrifice for our sins. Dear friends, since God so loved us, we also ought to love one another. No one has ever seen God; but if we love one another, God lives in us and his love is made complete in us. We know that we live in him and he in us, because he has given us of his Spirit. And we have seen and testify that the Father has sent his Son to be the Savior of the world. If anyone acknowledges that Jesus is the Son of God, God lives in him and he in God. And so we know and rely on the love God has for us. God is love. Whoever lives in love lives in God, and God in him. In this way, love is made complete among us so that we will have confidence on the day of judgment, because in this world we are like him. There is no fear in love. But perfect love drives out fear, because fear has to do with punishment. The one who fears is not made perfect in love. We love because he first loved us. If anyone says, "I love God," yet hates his brother, he is a liar. For anyone who does not love his brother, whom he has seen, cannot love God, whom he has not seen. And he has given us this command: Whoever loves God must also love his brother

1 John 4:7-21

This is a wonderful Scripture and easy for all to understand. We cannot love God without loving others. It is impossible! We cannot see a need and turn the other way yet say we belong to Christ. No, we cannot take care of all people and all needs, but there are people close to us that we can bless. My mother, grandmother, sisters, and aunts are all givers. My closest friends are givers. My kids are givers. I admire and am drawn to givers.

Our children are always watching us. As they observe godly behavior in us, they will grow up and become a blessing to others as they imitate what they have seen. This is good, and this is God's plan to pass the blessing on to the next generation. Amen and amen!

I ask that we love one another. And this is love: that we walk in obedience to his commands. As you have heard from the beginning, his command is that you walk in love.

2 John 5-6

Everyone who believes that Jesus is the Christ is born of God, and everyone who loves the father loves his child as well. This is how we know that we love the children of God: by loving God and carrying out his commands. This is love for God: to obey his commands. And his commands are not burdensome, for everyone born of God overcomes the world. This is the victory that has overcome the world, even our faith. Who is it that overcomes the world? Only he who believes that Jesus is the Son of God.

1 John 5:1-5

Part 2

The following sayings or incidents are actual events that went on in the lives of my siblings and me and my mother and grandmother. We were not actually sat down and taught these things but their repetition in our house were taken into our minds and all these many years later, we have not forgotten.

We were going to celebrate my mom at one of our many family reunions, I put out a call for everyone to e-mail quotes or sayings or events that they remember going on in our house and they possibly have repeated those things in their own homes. It was amazing all the things that were sent to me and either jogged my memory or confirmed events that I had already added to the book. I only put the ones in the book that I could personally remember myself. It amazed me the way that I could start one of the saying and someone else could say a sentence and then I could say a part or two and then a third person could say another part or two.

These made me think of the many others things our kids learn and pick up by the repetitions that go on in our homes. I know this takes us back to the chapter on things we make common to our kids. We are being watched and we can accomplish so much with the responsibility of guarding our thoughts, our mouths and our actions. I have also read an interested article regarding the effects on our offspring by our diets and our habits or indulgences. We have a wonderful and grave responsibility to the next generation. Eyes are watching us to form their beliefs, likes and dislikes. I think it is funny to ask a child why they do or do not do the things they do and the only answer they can give is their mother, father, grandparent, sibling, neighbor, teacher, church member, etc., did the same things when they were younger. That behavior, good or bad, triggered something in the young person to want to behave in like manner.

My family is African-American and from the South, therefore many of the statements will mean nothing to most people but the point is that we still know these things at 40 and 50 plus years later. My point is to show the influence parents have on their kids. If we take time, like the scriptures says, and teach our kids about the Bible and God, imagine the effects this could have on generations to come. This must start when they are young. It cannot start when they are teenagers for it will probably be too late at that time. The world and its influences will have already made it argument against all the Bible has to say. It has already started to make them feel they must agree with the majority and they will be called intolerant. We have a right to believe in God and stand for the things we believe. What is happening in America when my rights as a God fearing, Bible-believing, truly living it Christian are trampled on and it is ok?

We are truly a product of our environment!

You could be Carrie's child or grandchild:

If you know that Proverbs 3:5,6 says *"Trust in the Lord with all thy heart and lean not on your own understanding; in all your ways acknowledge Him and He will direct you path."*

If you've heard the phrase 'You've got a head like Collin's ram!'

(You didn't do something you were suppose to do but I don't know who is Collins or his ram)

If you've shared a bed with more than 3 or 4 siblings and somebody wet the bed and made everyone miserable!

If you've had that index finger pointed at you, and you knew what that meant.

If you've worn a stinky tallow cloth for a chest cold or had turpentine on an onion under the bed to reduce fever!

If you've heard and enjoyed her singing 'Calvary, Calvary, surely He died on Calvary!

If you've had castor oil, mineral oil, cod liver oil, asphisada?, cocoa quinine, Geritol in hot cocoa, 3 drops of turpentine on a teaspoon of sugar, Father Johns and Epsom salt!

If she told you to put two broom straws criss-crossed in the baby's head to stop hiccups, give the baby's catnip tea to bring out the hives, and put a fifty cent piece on the navel so that it won't poke out!)

If you slept outside on the back porch on Jackson Street and had such an adventure looking up at the stars?

If you had ice cream in your oatmeal and jelly in your grits!

If you heard that 'a hard head makes a soft behind'!

(That meant you were going to be punished for misbehaving.)

If you heard the phrase 'Don't let your mouth write a check your behind can't cash!'

(Don't say you will do something and then you can't fulfill the promise.)

If a question was asked and you really didn't need a response, the answer would be 'lauro catch a mellin'!

(You knew to leave it alone at that point! It also meant it was none of your business)

If you know about getting saddle oxfords for the beginning of school but we called them bucks.

(Every year these were bought at the beginning of the school year. You stuffed them with paper, if you got holes in them to make them last the whole school year.)

If you can remember boiling sheets in a cast iron pot in the back yard on Jackson Street!

If you slept in your cloths, you were told that you slept ready to roll!

If you know who Mr. Brown was!

(This was a thick belt that was applied to the bottom for punishment. If you were told to go and find Mr. Brown, it was like walking the plank on a ship.))

If you bathed in Octagon soap!

If you got your butt whooped at school!

(The teachers knew they need only call her and she would correct any behavior on the spot. Most time the threat would suffice but some of us, like me, would not bend and she had to make the trip anyway.)

If you were asked often 'Do you trust Him? Also, if you were told 'it is God who works in us.' Also, 'it is our work to believe on Him, who He has sent.'

If you know she will get the 'butter from the duck'

(I don't know if you can actually get butter from a duck but this meant you were in trouble.)

If your mom would parade 15 or 20 kids to the civic events, and take you to the circus, parades, picnics, etc. to have fun.

If you prefer your biscuits with cane syrup!

If your mother would go outside and played softball or dodge ball or roll- and- hit –the- bat with her kids and the neighborhood kids!

If you were told that your siblings were your playmates!

If she made Vogue dresses for her daughters, granddaughters and nieces!

If all your brother and sisters jump in all of your fights!

If you've heard, 'it hurts me more than it hurts you.' Yeah, right!

If you had to give her a kiss before you left for school!

If she can make peach cobbler that compares to no other!

If she loves and cares for you dearly because you married one of her kids!

If you know the song, 'Ham bone", as you slaps the side of your thigh!

If you know the song. "There always somebody talking about me, but really I don't mind. They try and stop and block my progress, most of the time. The mean things you say don't make me feel bad, cause I got a friend like I never had. I got Jesus and that enough! He saved me! That's enough! He raised me! That's enough!..."

If you know the phrase,' you can attract more flies with honey than vinegar!

If you know the real meaning of 'Grandma's hand!

If you know a little song that went—' Had a little house up town, come around and see me, get your breakfast foe you come, bring you dinner long and tip out before suppertime, tip out before suppertime, hey little girl, you look so sweet, two little eyes and two little feet, cutest little thing, momma ever did see, tip out before suppertime!

If the poor woman couldn't enjoy an apple without eight folks wanting some and she would cut small slithers and hand everybody pieces!

If she inquired about your day with, "what's on the rail for the lizard!

(The meaning is -what's happening in your life.)

If she warned you about selling 'wolf tickets!'

If she would give a toast that went,' Here's to you, as good as you are. Here's to me, as bad as I am. But as good as you are and as bad as I am, I am as good as you are as bad as I am!

If she has an honorary degree from Spelman!

If she is listed in the Who's Who in Macon for black women!

If she sold doughnuts for you to win a camping trip and you did, sold dinners for you to win Ms. Ebenezer and you did, and wrote an eloquent prayer for you to say at graduation!

If you know the song,' God is still on the throne, within your bosom, you have, you have a home. And whenever you walk, you're not walking alone. Remember God is still on the throne!'

If even though it was your mother, your dates were still afraid!

If you knew how to sew an outfit and cook collard greens before age ten!

Pass the Blessings!

If you could potentially be awaken for not cleaning the kitchen before you went to bed!

If you were bounced yourself or did bounce your own children to the tune of 'doooo, ditty loo, ditty loo, ditty loo, ditty loo, ditty loo, ditty loo, ditty loo, ditty loopty,..'

(This tune was so loved by my kids! At around six months, they would smile and bounce continuously in my lap.)

If you went to church on Sunday, Monday – Choir rehearsal, Wednesday- bible study or pray meeting, Friday – comfuss (conference) meeting, Saturday – Mission meeting!

If she bought baby chicks for you at Easter time and colored eggs!

If you went sneaking up to the corner store to call some boys and got caught!

If she visited your school regularly and was often head of the PTA.

If you had a silver Christmas tree and a multicolored revolving light that sat on the floor!

If you know how to shell peas and shuck a sugar cane!

If her mother would say, "This hand hadn't ever felt any better!"

If her father was always there to give you a ride to school or from school, if it was raining!

If Ms. Goolsby was your first Sunday school teacher!

If you had a good hot breakfast before you left for school!

If you've be told that a soft answer turns away wrath!

If you've heard of pot ash soap.

If you put cooked grits and chipped-up chicken in your dressing. Then she came towards you with the hand she had mixed it up with and said taste

If you know the song, 'I thank the Lord for bread and for meat. I thank the Lord for life so complete, I thank the Lord, deep within my soul. He is everything to me.'

If you know the game that starts – Carrie, somebody's calling your name, Carrie, they must be playing a game, Carrie, you're wanted on the telephone, well, if it ain't my honey, I sho' ain't home, it the city clock going – ding-dong, ding dong and tick tock, ding dong, ding dong and tick tock.

If you know the tune, '3-6-9, the goose drank wine. The monkeys chewed tobacco on the street post line. The line broke, the monkeys got choked, and they all went to heaven in a little row boat. Clap, clap (This was done while everyone was clapping their hands.)

It amazed me all of the chants, sayings, events, rituals, etc. were repeated and remembered verbatim by any given child of my mother. Parents we can change the world with our influence. The family unit is a very important entity in the life of a child. The power a father and mother have on a child is amazing and both are needed and important for a well rounded child. Both father and mother bring separate and important parts to the unit. I may not have had a father in the home but I did have my grandfather and some uncles nearby and definitely a good mother.

Part 3

The following poem was written over the span of ten years. In the reality of the chicken and the egg, the poem was before the rest of the book. The rest of the book was birthed from the poem. I felt I needed to give scriptural references and my experiences as testimony for what was expected of us as parents and a parent's mistake in child rearing (myself as example). I went back to school to get my degree in ministry so that I could understand the scriptures more clearly. I know I will never grasp it all in one lifetime but I will always be a student of the Bible and of God. I know it is a long poem and it may be called a story with rhyming words at this point. I hope you enjoy it and take in the conversations.

Pass the Blessings, Please!!
(The poem)

(child to parent)

Please, pass the blessings on to me.

I imitate you in all I see.

I need your example and your guidance.

Even though at times, I try to hide it.

Mom and Dad, I love you dearly

And from where you are, you can see clearly

I don't know what my future holds.

It is for certain; I'll reap what I sow

Help me to sow seeds for joy and success

When I honor you, my life will be blessed

I'm listening carefully to the words you say.

I'm watching, too, to shape my way.

Be mindful of your jokes, comments and such.

I adhere to your habits very much.

If you're smoking, I probably will too.

If you drink, that is just what I'm going to do.

You can't use bad language and tell me not to.

I'm probably going to do this just like you.

Pass the Blessings!

You hurt and disrespected your parents in front of me

Remember—an apple doesn't fall too far from the tree

Mom, as your son, I love the pampering feel,

But my future wife will be getting a raw deal.

Dad, you give your daughter everything I want

This very thing to my husband I'll flaunt.

Dad, do you hit my Mom and push her around?

Mom, do you talk about my Dad and put him down?

Mom, do you value yourself, cause I need to see that.

Stop letting him treat you like an old doormat.

Mom, are the clothes you wear – reserved and modest?

Or as for the imagination, there need be less.

Society will impact me but so will you, Mom.

I may try those things, but return where I come from.

Dad, are you not the leader and provider at home?

I need feet of faithfulness that do not roam.

Dad, I like to sit around and do nothing with you.

My days at home are so very few.

Before you know it, I'll have left your place.

Give me kindly this one small grace.

If only we could sit down and laugh and talk.

Pass the Blessings!

Or even just go for a casual walk.

It's not the activity but you that I desire.

You are the one that I most admire.

Are you a screamer or do you withdraw?

Do you cheat others and disregard the law?

Are you prejudice against those not like you?

You're affecting me because, that probably what I'll do.

People are not meant to be used as Kleenex

Used, tossed, move on to the next

For if I do this when I am grown

Most definitely, I'll be left all alone

I'm learning from you every moment of the day.

Please, take heed, I'm shaping my way.

Do you ridicule me and call me names?

Do you mess up and on others you put blame?

Are you hard, mean and indifferent at times?

When you hug me, is it truly an act divine?

Do you not work or put in 16 hours each day?

Do you have dreams or is it "come what may"!

Do you tell me to lie for you on the phone?

When I try this for me, you tell me it's wrong.

Well, which is it, cause I'm totally confused.

Time and again, I do this for you.

A few of these things are not good or bad.

It's their extreme, that makes me uncertain and sad.

Excessive spending, debt up to your ears.

Not saving a dime, collection calls you fear.

Teach me to save and balance a checkbook-

Teach me when married, on others I don't look.

Teach me to cherish and spend time with my kids.

Teach me when to keep and when to get rid.

When certain indiscretions become common to me

Then!?, they are not wrong, as far as I can see

I've seen them practiced, day in and day out

Unless God intervenes, I'm taking this route

Teach me to love, show patience, and forgive.

Model the life that God wants me to live

Teach me and show me about Jesus Christ.

Cause otherwise, you're just throwing dice

————————————gambling with my life

————————————uncertain pain and strife.

Teach me to trust Him, knowing His Word is true.

So in good and bad times, I'll know what to do.

Teach me about Him day and night.

In the lowest times and the highest height.

For trouble will come, whether I know Him or not.

We're sinful man, and this is our lot.

But do I have to go through it alone?

I won't if you've rightly taught me at home.

When it's all said and done, it's my choices to make,

I'll stand alone before God, for my mistakes.

Please, pass the blessings on to me.

Show me the blessing of staying down on my knees.

To worship and praise the Almighty God,

And life won't have to be so hard.

(parent to child)

My child, in raising you, I've made many mistakes

The pain I've caused, I really hate.

I looked into your face when you were born

I thought of the gifts, on you I would adorn.

Gifts of material and immaterial things.

Only the best in life, I wanted to bring.

At that moment, I remember, I involuntarily inhaled.

These many years later, I'm waiting to exhale.

There are so many things that are not as good as they seem.

That will be the case a lot in mainstream.

For you to succeed – you must have self-control.

This will help you to reach all of your goals.

You can't hang on the fence, you must make a stand.

Being indecisive is a failure to plan.

A failure to plan is a plan to fail

You can do all things through Christ and you will prevail.

Lift your eyes to the hill from whence cometh your help.

Change and make improvements on all you were dealt.

I have to admit that there are joys and fears.

Through life, I'd be your guide for many, many years.

Pass the Blessings!

You won't know of all the sacrifices I've made,

And I don't mine making them for the rest of my days.

A lot of things I did were some trial and some error.

Not knowing the outcome caused me much peril.

Cause I didn't know either what the future would hold.

I just wanted to be there, to help you grow old.

You see, electronics and games and even learning to cook.

They all come with their own instruction book.

Day after day, I tried to figure things out

Not knowing for certain, if I was on the right route.

You were given to me for a limited time

Your purpose in life, I wanted to help you find

I'm sorry for not always setting a good example.

My regrets and remorse are so very ample.

I know it seemed to you that I was being real hard.

But your mind and your body, I was trying to guard.

I should have been careful of the things that I said

I should have been careful of the things that I did.

I didn't know back then, you'd imitate me

I didn't know you took things in or to what degree.

I should have thought of what I was making common to you

The things you saw, you eventually do.

I had things going on at various times

My own-way-in-life, I was trying to find.

I'm not trying to make up an excuse,

But peace and forgiveness, I'd like to induce.

Give birth to love and understanding toward me.

Let's pray that God will set us both free.

Satan, would love to set up strongholds in this

We hold on to unforgiveness- at such a great risk.

He'll have us bound by issues from the past.

We'll be distracted with things that won't last.

Let's talk things out, and never rehearse

Let's work together and put our relationship first.

(child to parent)

I'm sorry Mom; I can see that you tried

I couldn't see then, what you carried inside.

I apologize, Dad, for giving you grief,

I should have given your spirit relief.

What would hurt me then would hurt you, too.

Oh, the things that I said and the things that I'd do.

I was angry for not always getting my way,

But if I had, I wouldn't be here today.

I didn't like the boundaries you set for me.

I wanted to be wild and I wanted to be free.

I wanted to do things like all my friends.

It seemed so much fun,- living in sin.

I wanted to wear all the latest fad,

But you stood firm, and my soul is glad.

You don't know the pressure of one of my days.

If you really knew, you would stand in dismay.

My day doesn't end when I leave the school.

Pressures from on-line are part of the duel.

Face book and My space get a lot of my attention.

Many of my hours are taken since their invention.

When we're out together; my phone rings or there's a text

I don't understand why you are so perplexed.

I'm just responded back to my friends.

Being inconsiderate is not what I intend.

I want to open up freely without fear I'll be chastised.

My mind and my body, wants you to hear my cries.

Of all the words I listen to, I value yours the most.

Being a confused teenager is my only diagnose.

Thanks for not listening when I said 'I hate you',

You stood firm with me and I'm so very grateful.

Thanks for your prayers, chastisement, and protection.

I wouldn't know peace, discernment and correction.

I know you're taking care of me and I'm living in your home.

When I hear this over and over, it's like a metronome.

There are rules in your home and I know I must comply.

You were young once, so you can identify.

I know a small part of my life is my teenage years

But this does not calm all of my fears.

Times were good and times were bad.

But we were all each other had.

I'm glad you weren't one of those off –hands –parents,

Pass the Blessings!

I would have done things that were all too inherent.

My family maybe breaking up and ending in divorce.

My lack of calm and stability, this will only reinforce.

It seems like my world is spinning round and round.

This may be a next step for you, but for me – it's so profound.

I don't want you to stay in a situation that could jeopardize our lives.

And our love, peace and security are wrongfully being deprived

It's not good for me to see one parent treating the other one like dirt.

Both of you are important to me and these actions really hurt.

Is it possible to try counseling, before the union totally dissolves?

It isn't just the two of you; there are more of us involved.

The two of you may have grown apart but can't you reconnect?

If this is not possible, then can you show each other some respect?

I don't know the whole story; it will be different from you both.

What will this example teach me about keeping an important oath?

If only each of you would admit to their own specific part,

Then pray and work together and make a brand new start.

I may be living in a dream world and you'll say I don't understand

I need your example on how to live together as woman and as man.

Unfortunately, this decision, I am destined to repeat.

As I enter into marriage, it may be bittersweet.

I will enter with the intention of staying for better or for worst.

I will fight the tide of making this a generational curse.

If this decision has been made, and it is now a part of our lives.

Then hopefully with prayer, my future marriage will survive.

I want to learn and to grow from the lessons you've invested.

And live my life as the Bible has requested.

Being human, I have battles from within.

You took me to church, to know Jesus as my friend.

He is my God- from whom all blessings flow.

They were not in vain – all the seeds you did sow

So.., my life won't be perfect and He didn't say it would be,

You've done your part, let go and be free.

(parent's prayer)

This child is a gift that was given to me.

Please help me to raise them so they can succeed.

I want to do right by them but sometimes I don't know how.

I must keep my eyes on You and my knees must bow.

Even as babes, they were something to behold.

Unique in their own way and many wonders to unfold.

Some will say,' What have I done to have this blessed child?'

Others will say, 'This is what I get for being young, loose and wild.'

Unfortunately, there are others who have suffered ugliness and shame.

God loves all the little children and they are mine, He exclaims.

Thank you that your mercy for me is new every morn.

I need to share this with my child long after he's not a newborn.

A father and a mother are important in their children's lives.

When one parent is missing, then the child is deprived.

In either situation, please be what my child needs.

Some may physically be around but there is still no guarantee.

Help me to show them love and always keep my priorities straight.

In listening and spending time with them, our relationship to cultivate.

Help me see their talents and listen to their dreams.

The things that I may think is best may not be what it seems.

Pass the Blessings!

Show me when it's good to say yes and when to say no.

I don't want their lives to be a tale of sorry and of woe.

I know they must go through things to build up character and strength.

But some situations can give their lives fortitude and length.

Children honoring authorities is something that you require.

Blessings upon blessings will always surely transpire.

Help me to imitate you and be a good example to them.

I desire for them to love your ways and not to loathe and condemn.

I know I must let go of them or even push them out of the nest,

To figure out their own way, that you desperately want to manifest.

I want so much for them to love You, Lord, as I've tried to demonstrate

But whether I have succeeded at this is sorely up for debate.

There were times when I truly meant well in plans I tried to implement

Unfortunately, the outcome was not as planned, yes, this I must lament.

Help, me as I study Your Word to show myself approved.

I want to teach them right from wrong, then their follies they'll remove.

Only You, Father, can bring the needed peace between the two of us.

I feel my heart will break in two when we argue, fight and fuss.

Hear my prayers, oh God, for I cannot raise this child alone.

I want to have your guidance, so I'll stay humbly near your thrown.

(Child's prayer)

Lord, I want to do right but lust and temptations are there

Peer pressure and other things are giving me a scare.

I know my parents think there has been a case of identity theft.

Because I know I don't always act like myself.

Emotions and opinions are pulling me from side to side.

Sometimes I just want to run away and hide.

I feel like my parents don't understand what I'm going through.

So I talk to my friends whom I feel might have a clue.

I guess I forget parents have been down these roads.

With my mouth and actions, I sometimes explode.

They push forward – I push back!

I know down inside, I'm on the wrong track.

Yes, I know there has to be better ways than the ones that I am choosing.

When we both want to win, we will only both be losing.

Can we just slow down and try to compromise?

I want to open up freely without fear I'll be criticized.

I know what scares my parents is my childish immaturity.

They want to keep my mind and body in a state of purity.

Right now for me, that may not be what I sincerely want,

As I listen to them talking, I'm so very nonchalant.

Please, forgive me, for my awful show of disrespect.

It's your desire for us to come together and try to connect.

I need to show behaviors that earns and build their trust,

Instead of having tantrums and whining that things are not just.

Help me to stop saying, 'That's not fair.'

As I watch others families and try to compare.

I just know what I really want is to have lots of fun

To try new things, new places or even meet someone.

Of all the words I listen to – I value theirs the most.

Being a confused teenager is my only diagnose.

I want to listen to them and try to understand

Cause despite what it seems, there really is a plan.

No matter the circumstance, God, you knew I'd be here

You also knew of the situations, I'd be reared.

(Jesus speaking to parents)

Being fruitful and multiplying has been My desire.

But the family, as I planned, has been under fire.

There is so much division between fathers and mothers.

It causes confusion between sisters and brothers.

Children are not being conceived in love within the bonds of marriage.

People are coming together with so much baggage.

I would love to join with you to sort things out

And I would be with you from beginning and throughout.

The choice of marriage partners are soo… matter of fact.

And regretfully down the line, you'll see the impact.

People are chosen for Loneliness and Looks and Lust.

And if a child is conceived, then they feel that they must.

But of all of those 'L's, was true Love involved?

Then marriage is chosen as a matter of resolve.

This wasn't the way that I wanted the union to start

But if selfishness is laid down, My love I can impart.

I was not caught off guard when you made your decision,

But God still has a plan and I will be your liaison.

Yes, the decisions that are made will affect many more than you.

Grace and mercy will be yours if you choose them to pursue.

Grace is when you get what you didn't deserve.

Mercy is what you didn't get - cause God helped you swerve.

My plan is to prosper you and give your heart hope.

I want you to succeed and not to just cope.

If you succeed, then you can help your children, too.

Together, I'll help you all to be firm and to pull through.

Do not let yourself be anxious about anything

For by prayer, the peace of God is what I will bring.

Do not be conformed to the things of this world,

Yes, out of your oyster, I will bring forth a pearl.

All that you see is what's on the outside

There are gifts inside you that are trying to hide.

Just like the pearl, they must be diligently sought out

I'll make your path clear, there will be no doubt.

I'll call them forth, so that you can be a blessing.

I'll make them known to you and you won't have to be stressing.

Beloved, I have not given you a spirit of fear

I love you, My child, I want you to come near.

I have many things that I need for you to learn,

My ways to adapt to and spirits to discern.

Love is the foundation of all of my Words

Pass the Blessings!

To obey is better than to say that you heard.

Don't tell your kids," They are not our kind."

All the races are mine, you will find.

All are mine and I am theirs,

If they accept me, they are also heirs.

Give the children your good examples to imitate,

Because there are many worldly ways to impersonate.

They won't have to go looking for them, they will seek them out.

Without you, they can't make it, there will be no doubt.

You have to be firm parents and not so much their friend

They need your guidance and correction in the end.

They have to know that your love is real and your acceptance is true.

Let them live out their dream, not the one that was place in you.

Watch over their innocence and be diligent about that,

Guard their mines and secure their habitat.

Listen to the words on radios, movies, computers and DVD's

They are also in books and on T.V., games and MP3's.

The enemy and the world want to have them at all cost.

It's My desire that you won't have to suffer that lost.

Seek Me, first, instead of clubs, dance, and sports.

You'll be less likely to see them in the judicial courts.

Bring them together with others that believe.

It takes a village to raise a child, so that they won't be deceived.

Show me your friends and I will tell you about you.

Inevitably, you and them will have the same point of view.

Teach them to place the Word in their heart,

And when they are old, they will not depart.

Love each other and learn to forgive

This is the way that I want you to live.

For in letting others go, you set yourself free.

It doesn't matter if they choose to agree.

As far as it lies with you, there must be peace.

Your burden will be lifted and you'll feel the release.

I'll have lifted those heavy trials off of your back,

You were never meant to carry them alone, in fact.

Be anxious for nothing and make known your request.

When you search for me, I will manifest

I've searched your heart and I know your anxieties.

Accept My Comforter, and put your mind at ease.

(Jesus to child)

My command to you was to honor and respect

It is their job to discipline and correct.

Over you, my child, I told them to guide and to teach

Yes, you have to listen to speech after speech.

A lesson taught once will not do its job.

Your earthly side will surely rob.

It is not natural for you to do as you should,

Constant lesson must be taught until you've understood.

Your mother carried you and delivered you into this world

The pain was the same, whether boy or girl.

Delivery is a near death to her every time she gives birth.

But she constantly does it and fills the earth.

Dads that obey Me should work and provide,

Love and take care of you, in and outside.

I've instructed parents not to hurt or to provoke.

Respect people in your home like you do other folk.

When parent gets angry it's not always your fault,

The tension between you – must come to a halt.

There were times you got off track and you knew you did wrong.

The words of my book are to all my love song.

Pass the Blessings!

I love you so much, it makes my heart ache.

I know who's sincere and I know who's a fake.

Let not your heart be trouble neither let it be afraid.

All things work for your good when you have obeyed.

Life and death are in the power of the tongue.

Your mouth can set in motion, things that will be done.

Your body is my temple, you are not your own.

The world will tell you to yield to your hormones.

You shouldn't awake love before it's time.

Innocence and chastity are often undermined.

You've experienced things too early for your ears and eyes.

When this happens, some of your youthfulness dies.

You have plenty of time to grow and learn

Certain things right now – you shouldn't yearn.

If in marital situations, you let your mind submerge.

It is definite; you'll get that sexual urge.

Enjoy your youth and the pleasures it provide.

Love simple things and be satisfied.

The older you get, your life will have more commands,

What you need from Me is supply and demand.

Before there's a need, I have already supplied.

Pass the Blessings!

You don't have to perform, you are justified.

Be careful of the people you choose to hang around,

They can make your life, such a battleground.

Show me your friends and they will tell your story.

They can be your destruction or your crown and glory.

Choose friends that help you as iron sharpens iron.

Others will use and scatter you up just like a dandelion.

As a young person, so many are fighting for your attention.

It is up to you whom you give your cooperation.

Some choices seem fun but they are life and death,

And they may literally cost you your very last breath.

Study My Word and listen to My sages,

Going it alone is very outrageous!

There is protection in seeking advice from the wise.

Yes, and sometimes this will come from your family ties.

Your friend's interests are selfish unlike those of your loved one.

Don't waste parts of your life like the prodigal son!

Look around as he did and realize your predicament.

This is not your lot and it should be evident.

I have good plans for you and there should be no doubt.

There will be times when you have to do without.

Things won't always be easy and may involve a little pain.

Godliness with contentment is so much gain.

Life won't be easy all the time but I won't leave you alone.

I'll continue to walk with you even when you're full grown.

If there's a distance that comes between us, it will be one you have created.

You're the apple of my eye, one that I adore, and you - I have vindicated.

Trust in the Lord, with all of your heart and lean not to your own understanding.

I've known your past, you present and your future, with me you can do anything.

Take responsibility and know there are consequences for all of your thoughts and actions.

For every deed done, good and bad, there is always a separate transaction.

Especially designed with you in mind – in you I have planted a seed.

When you live in my plan and not the world's demand, your success is guaranteed.